Toward Engaged Anthropology

Toward Engaged Anthropology

Edited by
Sam Beck
Carl A. Maida

Berghahn Books
New York • Oxford

Published in 2013 by

Berghahn Books

www.berghahnbooks.com

© 2013 Berghahn Books

Originally published as two special issues of *Anthropology in Action*,
volume 16, issues 2–3.

Library of Congress Cataloging-in-Publication Data

Toward engaged anthropology / edited by Sam Beck, Carl A. Maida.
    pages cm
  Includes bibliographical references and index.
  ISBN 978-0-85745-910-7 (pbk.: alk. paper)
  1. Anthropology—Methodology. 2. Anthropology—Philosophy.
3. Anthropology—Fieldwork. 4. Participant observation. 5. Applied
anthropology. I. Beck, Sam.
  GN33.T68 2013
  306.01—dc23

                                                      2013004351

British Library Cataloguing in Publication Data

A catalogue record for this book is available from the British Library

Printed in the United States on acid-free paper

ISBN 978-0-85745-910-7 (paperback)

Contents

Introduction
Toward Engaged Anthropology

Sam Beck and Carl A. Maida

What if we use theory and method to benefit the people we study by partnering with them to move towards a just world, one where inequities are reduced and there is greater access to knowledge gained from anthropological research? To reach this goal anthropologists must play a more intentional and responsible role in working with people, communities and movements – the stakeholders with whom research is carried out. While anthropologists continue to act as decoders of cultures that are different and look difficult to understand or appreciate by society at large, it is critical for us to become more instrumental. We must participate in generating and bringing about change. We must be engaged in protecting the most vulnerable from oppression and exploitation and support the empowerment of communities to improve people's lives. This is a role not comfortably taken by tradition-bound anthropologists; however, an engaged stance moves the application of anthropological theory, methods and practice further along towards action and activism. At the same time, engagement moves anthropologists away from traditional forms of participant observation towards a participatory role by becoming increasingly a part of those communities or social groupings that we normally study. The chapters in this book suggest the roles anthropologists are able to play to bring us closer to a public anthropology characterized as engagement.

Engagement is a concept now used by universities to address decades-long criticism from business and government sectors.

The complaint is layered and focuses on the invented failure of higher education at a number of levels. Foremost it is a criticism that universities have been unresponsive to the needs of society, government and the private sector. At the level of undergraduate education, pressure has mounted to fulfil obligations asserted as beneficial to the public interest. The concern has to do with what is judged as: (1) the inability of graduates to fit rapidly into corporate regimes; (2) poor skills development in writing, mathematics, science and technology; (3) little or no experience in and a poor sense of citizenship; and (4) a limited encounter with volunteerism, expressed as community service.

Universities have been challenged to become more actively engaged with society as a whole, rather than reproducing the semi-isolation of the academic enterprise. This has happened as public funding is being withdrawn from higher education, concomitant with universities' expanded contractual arrangements with government and private sectors for product development. These trends are reshaping university operations, but also the rationale for higher education itself. Knowledge production is employed to bring about greater management efficiency and to accelerate consumption at the local and global level. The emphasis is on leadership development, innovation and entrepreneurship, with traditional arts and humanities education utilized as methods to achieve these.

At the undergraduate level this has been an effort to engage students in learning the relationship between theory and practice by participating in the 'real world'. Ironically, community engagement education was a radical alternative to didactic learning. Community-service learning was developed to reignite undergraduates to participate in civil society and help improve the conditions found in rural and urban sites of poverty. Simultaneously, internship programmes were implemented to hasten students in the workforce when graduating, reduce the inefficiency of graduates searching for the proper job for their skills and passion, and helping students make the connection between classroom learning and the real world. Two different encounters are taking on significance in higher education.

First, internships are ubiquitous and are supposed to anchor theory in practice, applying theory through work experiences in various professional settings. Ideally, students learn theory in their normal course work and then use the internship to test theory in practice. This approach of course fails to recognize that theory is also generated in the work place. A few internship programmes enable students to theorize from their experiences, reversing the 'testing of theory in practice' paradigm and instead students are asked to produce theory from practice. For example, at Cornell University's Urban Semester Program in New York City, which is informed by an engaged anthropological praxis, the goal is to assist students in personal and professional development and prepare them for the world of work with the realization that theorizing is an essential part of practice. Moreover, this form of engagement provides students with a sense of relevance and demonstrates the utility of their education in the work place and society.

Second, community-service learning has become an increasingly valued engagement process. Here students are supposed to learn about underserved communities, more often than not communities of colour. They are encouraged to value voluntarism and practise good citizenship in the hopes that as they mature into adulthood they will continue to be engaged. As a result of service learning experiences, students may become attracted to careers in the public or non-profit sectors and thereby participate in developing civil society.

Another criticism is the monastic-like separation of the university from the issues that need rapid resolution, and must be understood through research and knowledge production. By developing a way to produce change in the process of knowledge production, greater efficiency and more innovations may occur. Participating in communities as partners, collaborators and members redefines higher education's roles and commitments.

To legitimize internships and community-service learning in the academy, these experiential pedagogies are tied to course work and discussed as part of a continuum of learning to which students are exposed. This tightens the relationship of academic work and community problem-solving, whether this form of learning takes place in a government agency, a place of business or a neighbourhood. Although the professoriate is increasingly teaching these kinds of courses, special co-curricular programmes have been developed to work with students engaged in internships and community-service learning, using experiential learning pedagogies, whose origins are centred in John Dewey's and Paulo Freire's educational theories; social constructivism/constructionism; critical, liberating and democratizing pedagogies; and ethnographic fieldwork methods.

Undergraduate education is progressively tethered to the world of work in a very different way than in the past. Preparing students for professions is increasingly the mode of undergraduate academic training. Internships and community-service learning are being integrated into student schedules and have become mandatory elements in acquiring jobs. Critical to this kind of learning are communicative and social skills, the capacity for reflection and reflective practice, and a complex process usually referred to as 'team work'.

Another major force in engagement is medical schools' efforts of engaging communities through translational research, namely through practical applications of scientific discoveries arising from laboratory, clinical or population studies. This idea was always a mission of Land Grant institutions, translating academic research for use and distribution to the wider public. Cooperative Extension programmes are supposed to put into action the research work carried out on university campuses. At present translating the findings of basic research into practice is taking hold in the biological, behavioural and social sciences. This has implications about how knowledge is produced. The underlying mode of generating knowledge is shifting and contesting common standards of scholarship and academic values. The idea that research must take place in splendid isolation as an individual pursuit and that scholars are the experts who inform change is being transformed. Engaged scholarship refers to teaching and research that links academics with communities that promote mutuality in knowledge production. According to Barbara A. Holland, Senior Scholar at the Center for Service and Learning of Indiana University-Purdue,

> Now, academic institutions must become participants in a highly complex learning society where discovery, learning, and

engagement are integrated activities that involve many sources of knowledge, generated in diverse settings by a variety of contributors. (2005)

Of course, the notion that research ought to benefit society has been an ideological position advocated for by progressive academicians for a long time as an approach that democratizes knowledge production.

Beyond the university, anthropologists recently focused on collaborative and continuous learning on behalf of knowledge-based work, specifically through pedagogies of practice found in urban community-based organizations, and in museum outreach, after school, out-of-classroom, internship, community service, and high school apprenticeship programmes. These practice-based pedagogies surfaced within a new economy based upon innovative technologies and their products, and new ways to deliver services. Rather than thinking linearly about innovation, John Seeley Brown (2006) understands 'design thinking' as matching people's needs to new technologies and services through a human-centred discovery process. This fits within Hannah Arendt's (1968) view of education as a way of providing future generations with tools for 'setting right' a world that is 'out of joint' and perhaps 'wearing out' as a result of prior generations' demands and uses. Robert Halpern (2008) understands how work-based learning activities permit youth to gain greater exposure to the adult world and develop habits of mind and practice grounded in a sense of accomplishment, personal responsibility and self-direction. Accessible spaces will then need to be created to promote learning beyond schooling where individuals are exposed to what Thomas Bender (2007) calls 'urban knowledges', namely professional, creative, and social forms of knowledge that help to define a new metropolitanism that is socially inclusive.

Unemployment and displacement due to structural economic changes resulted in profound economic and emotional consequences in twenty-first century cities and their suburbs. Life worlds associated with traditional middle-class occupations narrowed, and with them the promise of a 'successful' adult life course for those following closely to a traditional career path directed by trade union and corporate personnel systems, leading to a preoccupation with what Richard Sennett (2006) calls the 'specter of uselessness', or the prospect of skills extinction and the fear of being made redundant in the new economy. A dual labour market of segmented work frames these new conditions, characterized by a primary labour market of stable, high-paying jobs with good working conditions and chances for advancement, and a secondary labour market of less stable, low-paying jobs with poor working conditions and limited mobility. Richard Florida (2003) regards the externalities of the new economy of entrepreneurial urbanism as contributing to uneven regional development, political polarization, disparities in the wages of creative sector workers and those in the manufacturing sectors, and increased pressures on housing prices; consequently low-income workers and artists are being forced out of their communities. Allen Scott (1997: 336) calls for an 'active cultural politics' to circumvent the 'more regressive tendencies in capitalist cultural production', and Jamie Peck (2005) points to the 'cargo cult' logic of the urban broad-based acquisition of new crafts skill sets and the resulting creativity; Stephen Barley (1992) locates this creativity within the high-tech knowledge-based workplaces, which is essential to assure social inclusion. Engaged anthropological work in this area has focused on how tensions and conflicts between adherents of creative and culture-led urban regeneration and their critics play out within these domains in metropolitan regions, and discuss the various ethnographic perspectives on new craft skill development in late modern urban institutional life, including the struggle for power, social knowledge and social inclusion.

Another recent ethnographical focus is that of civic aesthetics in the contemporary transformation of global metropolitan centres and their cities and suburban neighbourhoods, with respect to variations in transnational mobility; risk and security; affluence and poverty; subcultures and identity; and the use of formal and informal public and neighbourhood spaces. A negotiated 'civic aesthetics' guides the physical transformation of urban and suburban neighbourhoods through the construction of public and private buildings, public parks, plazas and streetscapes, and large-scale community redevelopment projects. Although political and

business leaders are often the primary movers of these transformations, they are aided by environmental design and planning professionals whose expertise and standards of professional conduct
require the inclusion of selected citizen participation in developing plans and policies, through focus groups, charettes, public
hearings, and advisory committees. However, this 'top-down' approach has been contested by advocacy groups and citizens left
out of formal participatory processes through civic aesthetic re-
bellions, such as counter- or anti-hegemonic movements that include graffiti, community gardens, squatting and sweat equity
occupation of abandoned buildings and spaces, sit-ins and dem-
onstrations. Neighbourhood historic preservation started as one of
these movements; the movement for low- and moderate-income
housing is another ethnic and immigrant subversion, following
Appadurai's (1996) notion of the production of the 'ethnoscape' in
the global cultural economy. Civil society movements are generally responsible for spearheading capital redeployment and investment in abandoned or semi-abandoned urban-settings. Youth
and young adults, as early participants in such movements, will
often develop an aesthetic regime that opposes the dominant civic
aesthetic. The young rarely receive the recognition for having led
such movements, but instead are seen ubiquitously as a negative force that needs to be controlled, limited and even punished.
There is an ethnographic dimension to the understanding of the
multisided dynamic and developmental processes that frame the
two sides of the debate on the construction of 'civic aesthetics'.
One side of the debate involves local government commissions
and agencies and their interaction with citizens, typically on behalf of protecting the natural environment and maintaining the
uniqueness of the local landscape. However, these two goals often
end up being used for exclusionary purposes by communities
and municipal planners. The other side focuses on counter movements that usually struggle for inclusion in determining the nature of housing, design, consumption and community spaces. An
engaged anthropology now looks at how tensions and conflicts
between the global and the local play out within these domains in
the metropolitan regions undergoing these transformations, and
how the various ethnographic perspectives on late modern urban

institutional life can throw light on the struggle for power, social knowledge, social formation and social trust; and civic culture development.

There is little disagreement in modern anthropology that it is an intellectual discipline constructed to benefit humankind. However, much of the work carried out is based on a discourse internal to the discipline; is rather theoretical or descriptive in nature; or is the application of methods and theories for analysing and elucidating practical problems by experts. Many of these attempts of engagement result in text-based products or solutions applied by expert specialists benefiting institutions rather than society.

Much of anthropology is standardized as giving voice to the voiceless; translating difficult-to-understand socio-cultural systems into understandable concepts and language; or deconstructing policies to expose, refute and provide alternatives to inequalities. However, the kind of anthropology we are advocating for here is one in which partnerships, collaborations and mutuality are central to the work, and local stakeholders co-produce knowledge by providing their wisdom and expertise, even in co-authorship. Mutuality work should not be defined by extractive fieldwork. Much of our fieldwork methods are consumed by 'obtaining data'. What we suggest instead is to use fieldwork methods to enter into dialogue with community members and participate in their lives to improve their conditions that they identify as concerns that limit them. We do this by exchanging expertise, permitting self-understanding, and perhaps empowerment, to take place and by enabling communities to reach their own decisions without imposing solutions on them from the outside. This approach is very much in the tradition of Paolo Freire (1985) and adult literacy education where teaching and learning are the components of the research process.

For most anthropologists, the text is a prerequisite upon which professional advancement is built and hence inevitable. Non-textual expressions of anthropology are usually dismissed. If we can agree that anthropological fieldwork is an act of intervention, then it should easily follow that anthropologists in the field ought to have goals, objectives, strategies and agendas that determine what these interventions should look like and be sensitive to their impact 'in-context'. This is not only an aspect of the methodology or technique in carrying out fieldwork but very much about anthropological theory, method and ethics. We need to emphasize the idea of 'in-context' because participant observation is a dialogic process, one that is neither objective nor value-free. Anthropological research of this sort needs a constant process of reflection and a reflective practice that recognizes knowledge production as dialectically produced with partners, between researcher and researched. From this perspective, the notion of 'researched' is no longer a viable concept. By design, the researched, or research subject(s) in contextually based public anthropology are understood to have expertise of their own that the anthropologist is looking to extract in the normal carrying out of research.

Marcus observed a shift in ethnography, away from the study of culture and towards the process of knowledge production (2008). This recognizes ethnography as multi-sited, a process in which indigenous people are intentional partners in ethnographic projects.

Carl Maida's chapter underscores some of the essentials of community-engaged research carried out in Pacoima, California, where a consortium of institutions that included a local organization, institutions of higher learning, faculty and students sought to improve the lives of Pacoima residents. Engagement includes: (1) developing trusting relationships; (2) sharing information; (3) implementing mutual learning strategies through constructive dialogues with non-experts; (4) developing local-level leaders representing different constituents; (5) recognizing lay people's knowledge and their capacity to contribute to the research as equals; (6) including youth development through community-service learning; (7) consistent and regular consortium meetings with local-level leadership; (8) a long-term commitment; and (9) the sharing of resources.

Thomas Hylland Eriksen reveals the relationship between Scandinavian anthropology and the public through a public media discourse. In Scandinavian countries, the work of anthropologists is integrated within the functions of the state, as they participate in nation-state formation and national identity creation. As a result, Scandinavians participate in a reading culture tied to a healthy civil society. What academicians write in newspapers or what they say on radio or television influences the general public. In turn, public discourse impacts on public politics and policies. The boundaries between research findings and politics are continuously blurred. In his Norwegian example, Eriksen demonstrates how anthropologists are actively sought out by political parties to inform them on the Sami and other non-ethnic Norwegians and national integration policies.

Brian McKenna uses his academic expertise to expose the disguised relationship between Michigan State University (MSU) and the Dow Chemical Company. Due to its economic and political clout, Dow succeeded in penetrating both MSU and the state of Michigan. It is able to influence MSU's research agenda, turning the university into a 'knowledge factory' for its own purposes and limiting critical analysis especially of environmental issues. McKenna asserts that education for critical citizenship is undermined by the university's drive to educate for the job market. The recent economic calamity caused by bankers and politicians confirms McKenna's position that 'markets do not reward moral behaviour'. He unequivocally advocates for a social science (an anthropology) that is engaged and 'demands [an] unrelenting public voice about injustice'.

Early in her chapter, Judith Goode refers to a contradiction inherent in public anthropology, 'the drive to raise the worth of disciplinary expertise and stake a claim to authority in the world of policy elites', and simultaneously 'cogently offer critiques of the very institutions which are gatekeepers for public knowledge'. Her solution is to reframe issues to make them easier to understand, jargon free, and to ask questions shaped by the questions the public is asking while simultaneously tutoring the public to understand political economic complexities and how they are manifested and experienced at the local level. Goode's chapter provides a developmental chronology of anthropology as she experienced it, with a focus on power relations. It is power relations, according to her, that must be surfaced in the growth of an engaged and public anthropology.

Udi Butler discusses his work in Rio de Janeiro, which uses a dialogical anthropology to plan an action with young *favela* residents. Butler discusses power inequalities inherent in this kind of work, but instead of leaving it at that, he points us towards reflection, specifically in-context 'self-reflection' through which collaborative partners become sentient of the power relations in the process. Of course, this is Freirian 'conscientization' that leads to the development of critical consciousness. This kind of engaged anthropology is as much about process as it is about outcomes. If process is taken to central stage, then it is necessary to pay much closer attention to it and identify it also as a research product. In this sense research partners are intentional participants in the engagement process. By not recognizing partners as co-knowledge creators, we 'limit not only the kinds of anthropological products made but may also constrain the possibilities of dialogue with those we research'. This is riskier than extractive research methods or using the pretence of an objective and value-free approach.

As Butler points out, Sol Tax encouraged making anthropological knowledge useful to those being studied to 'solve a problem *and* to learn something in the process', coining the term 'action anthropology'. Much like 'advocacy anthropology', engagement provides for the growth of 'liberatory anthropology'. Under such conditions research also becomes an instrument for community organizing. Maida's chapter on participatory research in Pacoima provides a good example of this kind of work.

Raúl Acosta discusses an example of action and advocacy anthropology and points out the importance of the process-as-product feature of collaborative knowledge production in public anthropology. He states that under advocacy networks, in which 'stakeholders from contrasting backgrounds' highlight 'intercultural challenges, anthropologists can help explain current relations and processes within fluid structures in order to improve their practices and results'. This entails the role of the anthropologist as translator or interpreter and as mediator. Acosta uses the notion of the map and mapping as a product and metaphor, as a key in facilitating successful interchanges among stakeholders. Anthropologists are in the position of creating and interpreting maps with their informants. For Acosta, '[a]nthropological observations provide an understanding of the complexities of dialogues, linkages and relations across cultural practices, histories and contexts'. Cooperative mapping establishes social solidarity among participants whose diversity may not necessarily produce

common interests, but who may come to share a common discourse and values in the course of producing maps.

One central feature in collaborative knowledge production is
a vigilant levelling of power within the working group in which
the anthropologist is one member, especially difficult when group
membership is dynamic, fluid and in constant change. '[C]ollabo-
ration itself is an intense field of political competition for resources,
status, and power' (Fischer 2009: 228). According to Acosta, 'in an
evolution of democratic ideals and practice, advocacy networks
are reclaiming the public and places'. Acosta echoes Marcus by
observing that as anthropology moves into the public sphere, it
moves advocacy networks into new terrain 'by forcing governments and society at large to take them seriously, while avoiding
becoming static institutions. By mapping their actions and interactions, we are not merely describing spaces and relations between
their components, but also helping to shape them'.

Billie Jean Isbell complements Goode's autobiographical analysis of theory and method developments over the span of her anthropological career, providing a biography of what must be one
of the longest research projects, carried out by Cornell University
anthropologists for more than 50 years. It is instructive to understand the initial project as an aspect of the Cold War in which the
United States competed with the Soviet Union for the hearts and
minds of those areas of the world that were 'underdeveloped'.
This went hand in hand with efforts before the Second World War
to increase agricultural production in agrarian economies. The
colonization and expropriation of indigenous hands generated
the Vicos hacienda in Peru where 'Seventeen hundred serfs who
were close to starvation were listed in the lease as chattel'. Vicos
was identified as the research site in 1949, perceived as 'isolated'
and needing 'modernization' through the diffusion of U.S. agricultural techniques and 'democratic' constructs. Cornell University
purchased the hacienda with the intent of returning the land to
the indigenous population of this mountain region. Due to the
increase in potato production, after the introduction of 'improved
varieties, chemical fertilizers and insecticides' and after 'ten years
of commercialization of production', Vicos purchased the hacienda from Cornell.

According to Isbell, the project made visible to a broader public the terrible conditions of hacienda life and the subjugation of its people. Yet, this exposure seemed not to make a difference. By today's research ethics, this project was flawed from the outset. Yet, it does need to be understood within its own historic context, the hegemony of modernization theory and the assumption that scientific interventions could be imposed without the Vicosinos' consent. Stein's work, according to Isbell, concluded that while life for the Vicosinos improved, perhaps prolonging the lives of some, their regional integration declined. The larger forces at work in Peru left indigenous people in states of underdevelopment and subjugated them to exploitation. Still, the Vicosinos democratized their situation by 'being politically aggressive outside of Vicos', although it will remain unclear whether this was linked with the Vicos project, or with the wider forces of change that were underway during the life of the project.

Producing knowledge only for knowledge's sake is no longer enough, if it ever was. We require a global effort, one that moves anthropology beyond the production of texts alone and encourages anthropologists to collaborate and participate with people 'they study' to bring about changes that the people feel they need. This is not a matter of anthropologists working *for* such people. It means they are working *with* them, using their expertise, their wisdom, to inform the decisions being made by people employing their indigenous knowledge. Each chapter's author in this volume explores this 'working with' to both bring about change and advocate on behalf of their partners, while documenting this work.

We want to acknowledge Chris McCourt, editor of *Anthropology in Action*, who worked with us to publish these articles in the Special Issue on Public Anthropology. We are grateful to Marion and Vivian Berghahn for their continuing support and encouragement.

References

Appadurai, A. (1996), *Modernity At Large: Cultural Dimensions of Globalization* (Minneapolis: University of Minnesota Press).

Arendt, H. (1968), 'The Crisis in Education', *Between Past and Future* (New York: Viking), 173–196.

Barley, S. R. (1992), *The New Crafts: On the 'Technization' of the Workforce and the 'Occupationalization' of Firms,* Center for Advanced Human Resource Studies Working Paper 92-08 (Ithaca, NY: Cornell University School of Industrial and Labor Relations).

Bender, T. (2007), *The Unfinished City: New York and the Metropolitan Idea* (New York: The New Press).

Boyer, D. (2008), 'Thinking through the Anthropology of Experts', *Anthropology in Action* 15, no. 2: 38–46.

Brown, J. S. (2006), 'New Learning Environments for the 21st Century: Exploring the Edge', *Change: The Magazine of Higher Learning* 38, no. 5: 18–24.

Fischer, M. J. (2009), 'Emergent Forms of Life in Corporate Arenas', in *Ethnography and the Corporate Encounter: Reflections on Research in and of Corporations,* (ed.) M. Cefkin (New York: Berghahn Books), 227–228.

Florida, R. (2003), 'Cities and the Creative Class', *City and Community* 2, no. 1: 3–19.

Freire, P. (1985), *The Politics of Education* (Westport, CT: Bergin and Garvey).

Halpern, R. (2008), *The Means to Grow Up: Reinventing Apprenticeship as a Developmental Support in Adolescence* (New York: Routledge).

Holland, B. A. (2005), 'Scholarship and Mission in the 21st Century University: The Role of Engagement', http://depts.washington.edu/ccph/pdf_files/AUQA_paper_final_05.pdf

Marcus, G. E. (2008), 'Collaborative Options and Pedagogical Experiment in Anthropological Research on Experts and Policy Processes', *Anthropology in Action* 15, no. 2: 47–57.

Peck, J. (2005), 'Struggling with the Creative Class', *International Journal of Urban and Regional Research* 29, no. 4: 740–770.

Scott, A. J. (1997), 'The Cultural Economy of Cities', *International Journal of Urban and Regional Research* 21, no. 2: 323–339.

Sennett, R. (2006), *The Culture of the New Capitalism* (New Haven, CT: Yale University Press).

Expert and Lay Knowledge in Pacoima

Public Anthropology and an Essential Tension in Community-based Participatory Action Research

Carl A. Maida

A 'public anthropology', with its mix of critical ethnographic and participatory action research approaches, can help to understand and even frame the ongoing dialogue between practitioners of professional and lay knowledge concerning quality of life in global cities. Anthropological methods for understanding situational conflict, such as the extended-case method of Max Gluckman and the Manchester School (Evens and Handelman 2006), can bring ethnographic analysis and praxis to the various debates about quality of life issues, such as housing, education, health care and the environment, currently taking place in policy arenas in the more engaged communities, worldwide. Within these arenas, experts and laypersons have begun to resolve disputes over competing claims about the definition of an issue, and for equity and greater access to common resources, or public goods. However, there are vast disparities in knowledge as a result of perspectives, both professional and lay, that the various stakeholders in these arenas bring to the table. These disparate viewpoints can result in conflicts, and more often than not, 'bottlenecks' in carrying out stakeholders' plans on behalf of change. Those sitting around the table will hold professional or lay perspectives shaped by divergent occupational techniques, habits of mind and world images. Making sense of the ensuing conflicts as social processes emerging between and among the various stakeholders in a community will require an institutional analysis that derives from long-term field-work – one that takes into consideration the multiple experiences and cross-cutting ties of the participants in the policy arena.

This was my own experience over the past decade as a co-investigator on action research grants from the U.S. Environmental Protection Agency (US EPA) on behalf of improving the environmental health of residents in Pacoima, California, a low-income working-class community of 101,000 persons in the northeast San Fernando Valley of the City of Los Angeles. Employing principles of community-based participatory action research, I partnered with various community stakeholders to design and evaluate action research projects on toxic dumping, pollution prevention, childhood lead poisoning, and on understanding and reducing toxic risks. As a medical anthropologist trained in community-based programme evaluation, I led a cross-disciplinary evaluation team that worked together for over a decade, designing a participatory evaluation approach, which combines the conventions of participant-observation with the ethos of community-based participatory action research. Based upon these principles, the evaluation team provided a framework for reporting progress; developed guidelines for the report; provided both critical readings of preliminary and final reports with suggestions for revision and editorial help to shape each report as a whole. For each project, rather than taking the lead in summarizing a community-based action research team's findings and conclusions, the intent was always to maintain the integrity of each team's unique approach to carrying out the overall goals of the project and its own specific objectives and course of action, but also its own unique 'voice' in explaining the study results and their meaning.

Building Community in Pacoima

At the interface of expert and lay knowledge is the prospect of comprehensive community building through neighbourhood-based initiatives that bridge efforts in socioeconomic, cultural and physical development of urban communities. As a resident-driven process, community building values local knowledge and broad participation to revitalize the physical and social infrastructures of low-income neighbourhoods. An example of this is the work carried out in Pacoima, which was a largely African-American community until the mid-1990s and is now over 85% Latino. Pacoima covers six square miles at the base of the San Gabriel Mountains and is bounded by three major freeways. Pacoima has a small plane airport and is bisected by railroad tracks. Twenty percent of the residents live in garages or rental rooms in single-family homes; many live in extremely overcrowded conditions. In several areas in the community, residences are adjacent to commercial or industrial facilities. According to UCLA environmental health sciences professor John Froines, 'while Pacoima does not have the worst conditions in the city of Los Angeles, no other community has as many conflicting types of land uses' (personal communication).

Pacoima was established as a railside stop for Southern Pacific Railroad passengers in 1887 (Pitt and Pitt 1997: 375). From the beginning of the twentieth century to the Second World War, the area remained a community of small farms, vineyards and orchards. During and following the Second World War, aircraft and other assembly plants turned mostly inexpensive property into land valuable both for residential and commercial purposes. During the war, restrictions were relaxed to permit African-Americans to purchase homes in Pacoima in order to provide a workforce for the industry in the northeast San Fernando Valley. After the war, the area became a blue-collar community of mostly single-family homes with a predominantly African-American population. Low-income black families also began moving to Pacoima in the early 1950s, with the completion of public housing projects.

Jobs were plentiful for both low-income factory workers and more middle-class working families. However, change came during the 1980s and 1990s in southern California's economy as aerospace-related and automobile manufacturing, and consumer product light manufacturing left the northeast San Fernando Valley. These changes had an enormous impact on local employment in Pacoima and surrounding communities. It is estimated that half of minimum wage and lower wage manufacturing and warehousing jobs moved from the area since the signing of the 1994 North American Free Trade Agreement (NAFTA), which removed most barriers to trade and investment among the United States, Canada and Mexico. A large number of good paying jobs with benefits left the area with the closure of the General Motors assembly plant in Van Nuys, Lockheed's aircraft plant in Burbank and the Price Pfister plumbing fixture plant in Pacoima. Lack of jobs eventually led to the displacement of African-American families from Pacoima. Because of newly available inexpensive housing, Pacoima attracted recent Latino immigrants, many of whom pooled their earnings to rent or buy a house.

Pacoima endured multiple crises, including deindustrialization, trans-national migration and environmental degradation, compounded by the Civil Unrest of 1992 in Los Angeles and natural hazards, as the community was near the epicentre of the 1994 Northridge Earthquake. In many ways the trauma of the earthquake forced residents to acknowledge that their community's built and natural environments were degraded well before the earthquake. The shared experience of the disaster helped to establish a place-centred community identity among neighbours, many of whom had recently migrated into the area, as they reconstructed after the temblor. As neighbours set out to repair their homes and clean up their blocks, they also extended their helping resources to people in adjacent neighbourhoods.

Out of these often small efforts grew a number of community-based initiatives to improve Pacoima, including one that is the focus of much attention in this essay, a grassroots organization, called 'Pacoima Beautiful', which locals formed to help residents clean up the town but then grew to promote environmental education, leadership development and advocacy skills to residents, with an agenda of civic engagement with environmental awareness and community building. Since its beginning in the mid-1990s, Pacoima Beautiful evolved from a volunteer beautification committee comprised of five individuals to an environmental justice and environmental health, community-based, non-profit organization that operates through the support of a policy board consisting of residents as well as professional advisors.

Monitoring Pollution

Beginning in 1998, Pacoima Beautiful brought together residents; university faculty, including an environmental health scientist, an urban planner and a medical anthropologist; environmental and other organizations; university service-learning classes as well as representatives from governmental agencies to address environmental issues in the community. Being able to partner with experts in various fields served to expand the capacity of Pacoima Beautiful as well as build a valuable knowledge bank. As environmental health and environmental justice became a more prominent part of the work of Pacoima Beautiful it was necessary to enlist the support of those who knew how to address these issues. However, alliances across disciplines within the university, and those forged between academic specialists and the lay community-based organization and its resident constituency grew incrementally, as this case study indicates.

Pacoima long suffered from environmental neglect that can likely be blamed for the high rates of environmental health risks and the numerous sources of pollution throughout the area. In addition to freeways, the airport and a railway line, there are more than 300 industrial sites that have left contaminants behind or continue to pollute the air, soil and water. Pacoima is home to five US EPA CERCLIS (toxic release) sites, two of which are currently being remediated. In recent years, community concerns focused on the cumulative impacts from contaminants, such as lead in paint and in the soil, emissions from freeways, commuter planes, diesel from trucks and equipment, older 'gross emitting' cars, landfills and the widespread use of toxic chemicals.

By teaming scientists with community residents and youth, the organization created a network that gathered data to understand the effects of environmental hazards on health. The data collection was coupled with surveys of more than 2,000 residents and merchants. The approach is community-based and community-driven information gathering, following principles of community-based participatory action research (Field Museum 2006). Pacoima Beautiful worked with University of California, Los Angeles (UCLA) nursing researchers using community-partnered participatory

methods to reduce health disparities by training community members to function as lay health advisers to provide health education
to other residents (Kim et al. 2005). Much like Dutch 'science
shops', Pacoima Beautiful's research agenda on environmental
quality of life is based upon concerns posed by community residents and carried out with local universities (Sclove 1995, 1996).

To remain operational, the organization sought funding, with
the assistance of university scientists, from foundations and public
agencies with their own agendas, such as the U.S. EPA's environmental justice agenda, and the U.S. Department of Housing and
Urban Development's (HUD) healthy homes initiative. Partnerships have been essential to the organization's success. However,
at no time did Pacoima Beautiful deviate from its own agenda
and there was much foresight in planning well into the future so
that, as opportunities came about, the organization was ready to
take advantage of them. Strategic planning was an important part
of the work of Pacoima Beautiful dating back to its beginning in
1996. The prospect of partnerships with local non-profit organizations, including universities, and patronage from public agencies
and foundations inspired dialogues around planning Pacoima
Beautiful's future as a sustainable organization in a transmigrant
community during its early years – a time when the American
environmental movement was facing a national debate on issues
of population and immigration (Zuckerman 1999).

In 1998, U.S. EPA Environmental Justice Office provided a
grant to Pacoima Beautiful in partnership with university-based
researchers, which focused on increasing residents' awareness of
the consequences of toxic dumping within their community and
also moved Pacoima Beautiful's staff members and volunteers towards understanding their role in the environmental justice movement (Faber 1998, Gottlieb 2001, Bullard et al. 2007). Specifically,
the grant was used to expand the partners' efforts in monitoring
pollution, to educate residents through a newsletter distributed
through neighbourhood schools and to focus on the widespread
illegal dumping practices of local residents, businesses and others
who view Pacoima as a dumping ground. The EPA funding enabled a group of urban studies and planning students from California State University, Northridge (CSUN) to provide environmental

training to Pacoima Beautiful's Community Inspectors – residents who have learned how to identify the sources of toxics and pollution in the community and to understand the potential risks to heath – and to develop an environmental audit of the area.

At one of their meetings, the Community Inspectors took the students out to a number of sites where there was evidence of illegal dumping. This firsthand knowledge enabled the students to draft an environmental audit that dealt with environmental problems, industrial-residential relations, enforcement, land use and zoning. They discussed their draft with the inspectors, made modifications based upon the group's suggestions and developed a Spanish-language version of the survey. The students then mapped the sites of environmental pollution in Pacoima and entered the data into a Geographic Information Systems (GIS) database. The GIS is used to display results of the community inspector reports visually, and forms the basis of a website containing a map locating pollution risks and hazards which can be updated continuously and used for reporting purposes. The project was the first step towards Pacoima Beautiful's goal of developing an ongoing community monitoring system for toxic dumping, solid waste disposal, hazardous housing conditions, safety in community parks and residential areas, and environmental health and safety of residents. As a result of this initial partnership, Pacoima Beautiful undertook subsequent environmental justice programmes on behalf of mitigating the effects of lead in homes and toxics in the community.

Promoting Safer Homes

Pacoima has some of the oldest housing stock in the San Fernando Valley; it is predominantly single-family housing, with over 80% of these 22,035 housing units built prior to 1980. Neighbourhood Knowledge Los Angeles (NKLA), a project based at UCLA, developed an 'Early Warning System' used to detect neighbourhood decay by combining information from the City of Los Angeles Department of Building and Safety, Department of Water and Power and the Los Angeles County Tax Collectors Office. According to

NKLA, the lack of financial investment in a community and care-less property owners, specifically absent owners, raises a 'red flag' for deterioration of both neighbourhood and housing. Pacoima has ten at-risk housing developments while the rest of the LA City has an average of four at-risk housing developments. Substandard housing conditions are relatively undetected. Tenants are often friends or relatives of the single-family homeowners. The tenants may be willing to discuss their problematic housing conditions but are not willing to file reports against the homeowner. Further-more, maintenance of housing is done mostly by the occupants themselves, be it the owner or the renters, rather than by profes-sionals. This is a cause for concern when dealing with old housing, which may have lead and/or asbestos problems.

Although lead was banned in paint in 1978, many Pacoima resi-dents are potentially exposed because the majority of the housing units were built prior to this time. Additional paths to exposure are the number of children living in the housing and the degraded state of the housing. Children aged six and under have the highest probability of adverse health effects from these exposures because they are likely to ingest paint chips and dust that might contain high concentrations of lead. According to data collected by David Jacobs et al. (2002), about forty percent of all housing constructed before 1980 in the United States have some lead-based paint and twenty-five percent have significant lead-based paint. Pacoima Beautiful became interested in addressing the potential threats from lead in Pacoima when, in a February 2000 report, *A Needs Assessment Report for Primary Care Services I – The Community of Pacoima, City of Los Angeles, County of Los Angeles,* the Los Angeles County Department of Health Services (LAC DHS) estimated that there was the potential for more than 5,000 children between the ages of zero and six to have high levels of lead in their blood.

Currently, an estimated 310,000 of the nation's 20 million chil-dren under the age of six have blood lead levels high enough to impair their ability to think, concentrate and learn, according to the US Centers for Disease Control and Prevention (CDC 2008). Environmental lead exposure has been linked with an increased risk for numerous conditions and diseases that are prevalent in industrialized society, such as reading problems, school failure, delinquent behaviour, hearing loss, tooth decay, spontaneous abortions, renal disease and cardiovascular disease (Lanphear et al. 2005). Exposure to lead can occur from eating food or drinking water that contains lead, spending time in areas where lead-based paint is deteriorating and turning to dust or working in a job where lead is used. Some current sources of lead, largely of foreign origin, still result in excessive exposures and sometimes intoxication. These include certain folk ceramics, lead in candy wrappers, lead-soldered juice cans, jellied fruits packed in lead-glazed ceramic pots, certain patent medicines and some traditional home health remedies (Trotter 1998).

Research has shown that children exposed to lead poisoning exhibited emotional impairment characterized by impulsive behaviour and short attention span. In later years, lead-poisoned children are much more likely to drop out of school, become juvenile delinquents and engage in criminal and other anti-social behaviour. According to researcher Howard Mielke (1999: 62), a major concern for children's lead exposure 'is whether there is a source of lead dust in the environment'. Lead levels in soils are usually higher in cities, near roadways and industries that use lead, and next to homes where crumbling lead paint has fallen into the soil. Soil naturally has small amounts of lead in it, about 50 ppm (parts per million); and about 200–500 ppm of lead is commonly found in city soil. According to the EPA's hazard standard for schoolyard areas, lead levels that are equal to or above 400 ppm by weight in play areas and 1,200 ppm in bare soil in the remainder of the yard are considered hazardous for children.

There are indicators that Pacoima natural environment may exacerbate the exposure to lead dust, as the community is susceptible to high winds during parts of the year. Aerial photos show Pacoima as having the fewest number of trees and ground cover in the San Fernando Valley. Lack of ground cover is especially problematic on open spaces in the community because the dust particles scatter throughout the community. There is no vegetation along the railroad right of way or nearby Whiteman airport to buffer the community from lead dust exposure from transportation sources.

Pacoima Beautiful partnered with faculty members and students from CSUN in 1999 to survey the community's knowledge about environmental hazards and health with specific questions on lead. The survey results confirmed the assumption that the community lacked knowledge about health problems associated with lead. From the survey, two efforts were initiated. The first was a coordinated research project organized by Pacoima Beautiful, between 2000 and 2002, bringing together faculty members from CSUN, University of California, Irvine (UCI), University of Southern California (USC) and UCLA to understand the potential risks to health associated with lead in two high-risk neighbourhoods in Pacoima (Lejano and Ericson 2005). The second effort began in 2000 when Los Angeles County Department of Health Services (LAC DHS) and Valley Care Community Consortium (VCCC), a community health planning body, invited Pacoima Beautiful to participate in a four-year grant from the Partnership for the Public's Health (PPH), established in 1999 by the non-profit Public Health Institute and funded by The California Endowment to identify a public health issue in the Pacoima community and to build organizational capacity to address the issue. Through the grant, Pacoima Beautiful was able to purchase urgently needed equipment and increase the capacity of existing staff members by providing training on environmental health issues.

The research project with the universities and the efforts and capacity-building activities through the PPH grant resulted in Pacoima Beautiful starting the 'Safer Homes for a Healthy Community' Programme. The Safer Homes programme, which is ongoing, helps residents to create healthy homes for their families in order to reduce and prevent environmentally related health problems, including lead poisoning and asthma triggers, such as mould and moisture. In 2002, through LAC DHS, Pacoima Beautiful was invited to apply for and received funding for a pilot project through a scoping grant from the Washington-based Alliance for Healthy Homes, a national, non-profit, public interest organization working to prevent and eliminate hazards in homes that can harm the health of children, families and other residents. The scoping grant provided initial protocols for lead sampling in homes.

The grant from the Alliance permitted Pacoima Beautiful to hire four *Promotores,* who were mothers living in the community, to conduct sampling in 100 homes. The *Promotores* received extensive training from CSUN faculty members, LAC DHS, Healthy Homes Collaborative staff, Neighbourhood Legal Services and Esperanza Community Housing Corporation. The *Promotores* learned about the importance of intravenous lead testing for 0 to 6-year-olds. They also learned easy and simple ways to make changes in housekeeping activities to minimize lead exposures. Regarding regulation, they began to understand the legal responsibilities of landlords to maintain the homes in good condition to minimize the impact of lead. They were taught the methods and criteria for securing structural lead control or reduction opportunities for their homes and the need to use Lead Safe Work Practices. The four *Promotores* and three other Pacoima Beautiful staff were trained and became lead sampling technicians through an EPA course. Once the *Promotores* received sufficient training and had developed a comfort level with their roles, they began to reach out into the community. They visited the residents in individual and group settings and shared what was learned about lead poisoning prevention as well as asthma triggers and home health hazards. After some time, the community members learned to trust the *Promotores.* Through the Alliance for Healthy Homes pilot project, the *Promotores* met with 96 families, with 88 of the families completing the entire process; 34 of the 88 homes tested had high levels of lead. Much of the housing visited by the *Promotores* was severely overcrowded and degraded with multiple families living in single-family residences and ancillary structures, including garages and attics of garages. However, many of the owners of rooms and garages being used as rental properties were related to their tenants making it difficult for the residents to request changes. Most housing enforcement centres on tenants rights in apartments, not on tenants in single-family housing; and many residents were either unaware or mistrustful of the County and service organizations and the services they provide. In their discussions with parents, they learned that only about twenty-five percent of the children eligible for free lead testing through government assistance programmes were in fact being tested for lead. Many parents did not actively seek out blood testing for lead, partly because their physicians were not recommending that they do so. Moreover, health care providers did not inform parents about lead prevention and of the need to test their children who had not exceeded national thresholds.

The *Promotores* had provided a valuable service to the community residents. However, on their own they could not reach the numbers that needed to be reached. Therefore, Pacoima Beautiful, in partnership with VCCC and LAC DHS, actively sought ways to expand the knowledge base throughout the community. First, the Alliance for Healthy Homes, through its Community Environmental Health Resource Centre, provided funding to Pacoima Beautiful to implement a rigorous dust sampling protocol, based on EPA criteria, to work with 225 families in Pacoima over a two-year period. Second, VCCC formed an Environmental Health Committee, consisting of LAC DHS, Northeast Valley Health Corporation, a local federally qualified health centre, Neighbourhood Legal Services and other organizations that met regularly to discuss what was being learned about lead and lead poisoning in Pacoima. Third, the *Promotores* developed and refined their communication and presentation skills and, through the CEHRC pilot project, began outreach to groups of parents in most of the schools and parent centres in Pacoima. In 2003, Pacoima Beautiful, LAC DHS and VCCC hosted an Environmental Health Roundtable for 40 community stakeholders to share what was learned about environmental health issues. A primary focus of the Roundtable was lead and lead poisoning. The Roundtable produced a partnership to address lead issues in Pacoima. The first activity of the partnership was to apply for the EPA Collaborative Problem Solving (CPS) Grant. Writing the CPS grant proposal provided the partners with an opportunity to address specific issues with regard to lead and lead poisoning as well as serve as a device for sharing knowledge throughout the community. Pacoima Beautiful and partners based the project goals and strategy for the CPS grant proposal on the findings from both the work done previously by the partners and input from residents. The CPS grant focused on efforts to increase lead blood screening rates of children aged six and under. The project sought to integrate lead hazard control with other community efforts and also to clearly identify lead hazards in high-risk neighbourhoods and present workable solutions to reduce the lead burden. This would be done by analysing and synthesizing current data, and then convening a stakeholder forum regarding lead poisoning and community development. In addition, Pacoima Beautiful and its partners would participate in efforts to train the Los Angeles City Building and Safety Department effectively to enforce lead-safe work repair practices to pre-1978 housing and to educate contractors, workers, landlords and homeowners in lead-safe work practices, and work with City government to develop a housing registry for lead-free homes and apartments.

The work done through the CPS grant demonstrated a particularly high degree of success in dividing the above goals into detailed objectives that were each agreed to and achieved by one or more specific project partners or other stakeholders. In addition, these detailed objectives also were incorporated into a stepwise, detailed, comprehensive strategy for achieving each of the three project goals. The project was effective in encouraging the affected community to participate in the various activities that were presented in the project work plan. Much of this success can be attributed to the *Promotores* who provided a vital, two-way communications link between the project and community members. The project's success can also be attributed to the variety and depth of training and continuing support provided to the *Promotores* by the partners, who ensured that these lay health educators carried a high degree of knowledge about available resources for addressing a wide variety of issues in the community. In-depth knowledge of lead-related issues alone would not be sufficient to sustain the long-term, mutual value and trust between the *Promotores* and the Pacoima community. This sense of trust came about initially by convening all of the known stakeholders as part of the grant-writing process and reaching consensus on the nature of the problem and on how to conduct the project prior to its inception. Specific community input was obtained and incorporated into the grant through nine focus groups involving 105 residents. Moreover, the *Promotores* are trusted and accepted in the community, and are trained by other stakeholders to provide the abovementioned two-way link to the needs of the community and the solutions to those needs. As stated by Pacoima Beautiful staff member Patricia Ochoa, the 'level of trust and transparency regarding local environmental health issues is the most critical component in this process for the collaboration. 'Without this credibility, the other partners would have to expend considerable resources and effort to attain this level of trust' (personal communication).

Expert and Lay Knowledge in Community-based Participatory Action Research

The case example of Pacoima Beautiful's collaborative efforts on behalf of reducing toxic exposures in the community illustrates how local-level coalitions have allied business, government, non-profits and universities to implement planned change. Each aspect of the initiative was publicly discussed in meetings of Pacoima Beautiful's leadership and community advisory board, and among neighbourhood residents. Outside experts who participated in these environmental health initiatives have had to be sensitive to the autonomy and leadership issues involved in the community-based and resident-driven model embraced by Pacoima Beautiful.

In the above case, early identification of the issue by a community-based organization helped to engage others to address the issue and sustain the effort and make it grow. Pacoima Beautiful identified and worked closely with all stakeholders to reach consensus on the three project goals, which allowed them to collaborate on an effective strategy that integrated the unique contributions that were available from the numerous partner organizations. Following this was the need to identify appropriate partners. Each of the partners has different constituencies so that the work done to prevent lead poisoning was spread in many different venues throughout the community: university faculty took the information gathered by the *Promotores* and the federally qualified health centre and analysed and mapped the data; the health centre then provided information to its physicians, patients and specifically Women, Infants and Children (WIC) Program recipients; the County health agency and a regional 'healthy homes' collaborative provided technical information on lead screening tests and methods for lead exposure avoidance; the regional community health planning body provided the links to healthcare providers; and the regional legal services agency provided legal advice on issues such as landlord responsibilities and methods for improving enforcement of lead-free repair laws. In addition, the partners had the benefit of university-based evaluators who continued to evaluate the project during the process of planning and implementation.

Once identified, considerable attention was given to the clarification of each partner's role. Pacoima Beautiful took it upon itself to communicate actively and clearly with the partners at the outset of the project to eliminate any potential misunderstandings with respect to the project goals and other data that each partner might want to collect during the project to satisfy their specific needs. During these early communications, the organization's staff maintained their role as the key decision-makers with regard to project scope and direction. Throughout there was a need for frequent clarifications of the issue and potential resolutions. Pacoima Beautiful served as the clearinghouse for information and data and then would pass it on to the partners. In that capacity, the organization could keep the partners informed on the current status of their main objectives as the partners worked to attain their part in the project goals. In the end, the partnership stayed together through an EPA Community Action for a Renewed Environment (CARE) Program grant to identify toxics in the community, to address specific issues, such as the monitoring of all diesel sources in the community, and to extend the childhood lead poisoning prevention and abatement work into other communities. The partnership – of public and non-profit organizations, and of professional experts and lay advocates – is thus expanding its work beyond lead to include other toxic risks in the community, such as facilities listed in the U.S. EPA's Toxic Release Inventory (TRI), and is poised to identify potential toxic sites through site screenings in order to develop an understanding of the impact of toxics on the health of Pacoima residents.

Such collaborative planning of research design and methodology discloses unexplored strategies and solutions to existing problems and allows the residents to develop sensitivities towards the early detection of problems. The community-based research process that emerged from this style of foresight and planning involved the collaboration of lay community members and experts to produce new knowledge for social change (Murphy, Scammell and Sclove 1997). This practice carries on the work of community development researchers so influential in creating the philosophical underpinnings for America's urban agenda since the late 1960s (Warren 1971, Bennis, Benne and Chin 1985). As 'action researchers', they valued the involvement of community residents in all aspects of need and data analysis so that when action strategies are developed, the people most affected by their consequences will have a substantial investment in the action (Stringer 2007). Their approach to urban transformation also promises some assurance that community residents will continue to be participants over the long term.

Changing the Structure of University-based Expertise in Pacoima's Community Building

Although alliances between academic experts and lay advocates in Pacoima were strengthened with each successive (and successful) joint project, the structure of university-initiated consultation on behalf of comprehensive community building changed considerably over the period covered by the above case. In the decade following the 1992 Civil Unrest in Los Angeles, local universities became more involved in the affairs of their surrounding communities. However, these involvements were built upon the efforts by established agencies and institutions, outside of academia, that had sustained ongoing consultative relationships with professionals and residents within these communities well before the urban crisis. In Pacoima, individual university faculty members and their students initially reached out to local professionals engaged in community-building projects organized by the regional United Way agency in the years prior to the period of intensive federally funded crisis intervention. Following the 1992 Civil Unrest and the 1994 Northridge Earthquake, service agencies used a crisis intervention model to disseminate knowledge and helping strategies to meet residents' immediate needs and to reconstruct community infrastructure, including schools, health care and human services. The model, used by the Federal Emergency Management Agency (FEMA) after an emergency declaration, is top-down and short-term with the goal of returning control to civic and organizational leaders as quickly as possible. In communities, such as Pacoima, where the schools had become the centres of crisis response and rebuilding activities, and locales for the re-establishing of trust between professionals and residents as well, a school-based systems integration approach evolved. The incorporation of FEMA-funded activities within the existing network of the United Way-integrated services on behalf of community building in Pacoima only increased localized trust in outside helping efforts (Schomber et al. 2001).

As the systems integration approach gradually replaced the crisis-driven model, residents began to work side-by-side with professionals, including university professors and their students engaged in school-based activities, and paraprofessionals linked through collaborative activities in school-based parent centre programmes. Within this bridging network (Briggs 2003), all parties worked together towards common school and youth-focused programmatic goals within the existing educational system and local political structure, with the overarching goal of bringing about change from within the system. However, the school-based service settings, where collaborative partnerships had taken place in the years following the multiple urban crises, were facing severe budget cuts as the economic downturn of 2000–2001 began to affect public funding in California.

In the ensuing years, with the eventual dissolution of the more comprehensive outreach initiatives carried out with direct funding by the universities, which had emerged a decade earlier in the aftermath of civil unrest and natural disaster, the trend shifted to academic community-focused partnering. With publicly funded education, health care and urban services facing severe budgetary cutbacks, the university would contribute technical assistance, research and professional personnel, but no direct funds, to high-need communities like Pacoima. The idea being that such synergies would afford opportunities for training, service and research to help disadvantaged populations with political will, but very limited resources, to confront their economic, educational, health and other disparities. Faced with their own budgetary crisis, the universities thus pulled back their support for structural change at the community level. As a result, the more comprehensive university partnership initiatives rapidly devolved, from collaborative support of building community assets, to funding specific projects linked to individual faculty or staff members. Rather than working together with colleagues in multidisciplinary projects on behalf of a particular community, individual faculty members and staff members would now have to compete for funds and recognition as a 'community partner' aligned with a specific community-based project. In the end, this shift away from collaboration towards competition, between faculty-partnered projects and between communities, for scarce university funds, created a sense of distrust in the nascent university–community partnerships that had just begun to emerge in places like Pacoima. This breakdown of trust was highest among the many non-academic professionals who had sustained ties to local schools and agencies throughout a decade of civic crisis.

To realize the norm of collaboration promised by community-campus partnerships requires ongoing dialogue between community stakeholders and university partners about mutually determined priorities, strategies and policies. Moreover, these partnerships are optimally sustained around a common mission: that of service (Sirianni and Friedland 1997; Ostrander 2004). As it takes considerable time to build up community-scale initiatives, the university will need to sustain a genuine level of commitment for the duration, despite periodic budgetary crises, faculty turnover and gaps in specific project funding. The resulting culture of academic engagement (Cherwitz 2005) would also commit the research university to reconnect its scientific and public service missions through collaborative problem solving and community-based knowledge development. The university would then be poised to combine academic expertise and local knowledge on behalf of public goods, such as education, health care and the environment, that affect the quality of life in its neighbouring communities.

Acknowledgements

This study was funded by a grant from the U.S. Environmental Protection Agency, Office of Environmental Justice, Environmental Justice Collaborative Problem-Solving (EJ CPS) Cooperative Agreement Program – Agreement No: PS 831555-01-0 – Pacoima Lead Poisoning Prevention Community Project. I would like to thank Karen Henry, Charles Lee and Delta Valente of the U.S. Environmental Protection Agency, and also Kristin Aldana-Taday, Marlene Grossman, Guadalupe Hernandez, Elvia Hernandez, Josephina Hatamian, Patricia Ochoa, Nora Rangel and Liseth Romero-Martinez of Pacoima Beautiful. Thanks as well to Chris McCourt for critical suggestions and sound editorial advice that yielded a more coherent essay. I would also like to acknowledge the ongoing support and critical judgement of Sam Beck, who continues to inspire my work in public anthropology.

Earlier versions of some sections of this essay were published in 'The City is the Frontier', in *Pathways through Crisis: Urban Risk and Public Culture* (Lanham and New York: Rowman and Littlefield, 2008).

References

Bennis, W. G., Benne, K. and Chin, R. (1985), *The Planning of Change,* 4th ed. (New York: Holt, Rinehart and Winston).

Briggs, X. de S. (2003), *Bridging Networks, Social Capital, and Racial Segregation in America.* Kennedy School of Government Faculty Research Working Paper Series RWP02-011. Cambridge, MA: John F. Kennedy School of Government, Harvard University.

Bullard R. D., Mohai, P., Saha, R. and Wright. B. (2007), *Toxic Wastes and Race at Twenty: 1987–2007 – Grassroots Struggles to Dismantle Environmental Racism in the United States* (Washington, DC: National Council of Churches of Christ).

Cherwitz, R.A. (2005), 'Citizen Scholars', *The Scientist* 19: 1, 10.

Evans, T.M.S. and Handelman, D. (2006), *The Manchester School: Practice and Ethnographic Praxis in Anthropology* (New York: Berghahn Books).

Faber, D. (ed.) (1998), *The Struggle for Ecological Democracy: Environmental Justice Movements in the United States* (New York: Guilford Press).

Field Museum (2006), *Collaborative Research: A Practical Introduction to Participatory Action Research (PAR) for Communities and Scholars* (Chicago: Center for Cultural Understanding and Change, The Field Museum).

Gottlieb, R. (2001), *Environmentalism Unbound: Exploring New Pathways for Change* (Cambridge, MA: MIT Press).

Jacobs, D., Clickner, R. P., Zhou, J. Y., Vlet, S. M., Marker, D. A., Rogers, J. W., Zeldin, D. C., Broene, P. and Friedman, W. (2002), 'The Prevalence of Lead-based Paint Hazards in U.S. Housing', *Environmental Health Perspectives* 110: A599–A606.

Kim, S., Flaskerud, J. H., Koniak-Griffin, D. and Dixon, E. L. (2005), 'Using Community-partnered Participatory Research to Address Health Disparities in a Latino Community', *Journal of Professional Nursing* 21: 199–209.

Lanphear, B. P., Hornung, R., Khoury, J., Yolton, K., Baghurst, P. Bellinger, D. C., Canfield, R. L., Dietrich, K. N., Bornschein, R., Greene, T., Rothenberg, S. J., Needleman, H. L., Schnaas, L., Wasserman, G., Graziano, J. and Roberts, R. (2005), 'Low-level Environmental Lead Exposure and Children's Intellectual Function: An International Pooled Analysis', *Environmental Health Perspectives* 113: 894–899.

Lejano, R. P. and Ericson, J. E. (2005), 'Tragedy of the Temporal Commons: Soil-bound Lead and the Anachronicity of Risk', *Journal of Environmental Planning and Management* 48: 301–320.

Mielke, H. W. (1999), 'Lead in the Inner Cities', *American Scientist* 87: 62–73.

Murphy, E., Scammell, M. and Sclove, R. (1997), *Doing Community-based Research: A Reader* (Amherst, MA: Loka Institute).

Ostrander, S.A. (2004), 'Democracy, Civic Participation and the University: A Comparative Study of Civic Engagement on Five Campuses', *Nonprofit and Voluntary Sector Quarterly* 33, no. 1: 74–93.

Pitt, L. and Pitt, D. (1997), *Los Angeles A to Z: An Encyclopedia of City and County* (Berkeley: University of California Press).

Schomber, T. L., Anderson, J., Berger P. M., Brown T. B. and Zdenek, R. O. (2001), 'A Place to Go: United Way as Community Builders During Crisis Response', *Community* 4, no. 1: 20–25.

Sclove, R. E. (1995), 'Putting Science to Work in Communities', *The Chronicle of Higher Education* 41, no. 29 (31 March): B1–B3.

——— (1996), 'Town Meetings on Technology', *Technology Review* 99: 24–31.

Sirianni, C. and Friedland, L. (1997), 'Civic Innovation and American Democracy,' *Change* 29, no. 1: 14–23.

Stringer, E. T. (2007), *Action Research*, 3rd ed. (Thousand Oaks, CA: Sage).

Trotter II, R. T. (1998), 'A Case of Lead Poisoning from Folk Remedies in Mexican American Communities', in *Understanding and Applying Medical Anthropology*, (ed.) P. J. Brown (Mountain View, CA: Mayfield), 279–286.

US Department of Health and Human Services, Centers for Disease Control and Prevention, Lead Poisoning Prevention Program <http://www.cdc.gov/nceh/lead/>.

Warren, R. L. (1971), 'The Sociology of Knowledge and the Problems of the Inner Cities', *Social Science Quarterly* 52: 468–485.

Zuckerman, B. (1999), 'The Sierra Club Immigration Debate: National Implications', *Population and Environment* 20: 401–412.

Norwegian Anthropologists Study Minorities at Home
Political and Academic Agendas

Thomas Hylland Eriksen

In Norway, anthropological engagement with domestic political issues has been consistent (and complex) ever since Norwegian anthropologists began to do research among minorities 'at home'. Even the most meticulously descriptive, or arcanely analytic, research monograph on the Sami or on immigrants is bound to be interpreted, largely by non-academic readers, in a political context where issues of minority rights, national cohesion, multiculturalism and problems of cultural diversity have been at the forefront for many years. Anthropological studies are perused by civil servants (many of whom, in fact, have a training in the social sciences, often including anthropology), by NGOs and political interest groups and, occasionally, by a wider readership. The anthropology of Norway is, in other words, public whether the anthropologists like it or not. Some in fact use their position, and their research, in attempting to influence public opinion and policymakers directly. Many Norwegian anthropologists thus write for the press, appear on radio and television, and publish the occasional book intended for the general reader.

No anthropologist writing about ethnic minorities in Norway can afford to be oblivious of the political connotations of their work, and the boundaries between scholarship and engagement, or between research and politics, are continuously blurred. Naturally, there is considerable reflexive awareness of this among anthropologists working 'at home' although we, like any profession, have our blind spots, and besides, anthropologists often feel that they are being misrepresented and misunderstood by non-academics relating to their work. Since research agendas and journalistic or political agendas often differ, a frontier zone of negotiations and mutual misunderstandings, but also occasionally of fruitful collaboration and learning, has emerged in the area of minority research over the last few decades. This essay explores some of the ways in which the political and the scholarly merge, forcing scholars to become public anthropologists whether they like it or not. Let us begin with the indigenous Sami and the anthropologist.

The Sami are an ethnic group numbering roughly 40,000 in Norway (with smaller numbers in the neighbouring countries of Finland, Sweden and Russia). Although they are as diverse today as the majority Norwegians in their ways of life, Sami are symbolically associated with reindeer herding and transhumance (seasonal migration), an economic activity monopolised by (certain) Sami and invested with considerable prestige. Following a centuries-long period of Norwegianization (attempted 'acculturation' and assimilation), a modern indigenous rights movement began to develop in the 1950s and 1960s. Since the early 1980s, the Sami movement has achieved political recognition, leading to new legislation on land tenure and language rights, and the formation of a Sami parliament in 1990, with limited but real legislative power over the Sami core regions (notably Finnmark county, the northeastern corner of Norway).

Anthropologists and ethnologists have been involved with the Sami movement since the beginning of academic research in the country. Professor Gutorm Gjessing at the Ethnographic Museum in Oslo, the last cultural historian to hold this chair (social anthropology took over entirely from the 1970s), was responsible for the decision, as early as 1951, to move the Sami collections of the museum to the open-air Norwegian Heritage Museum (*Norsk Folkemuseum*), arguing that since the Sami were a Norwegian people, their material culture should be exhibited alongside Norwegian peasant artefacts and buildings (Bouquet 1996: 45). A strong political statement at the time, Gjessing's decision reflected his view that Norwegians and Sami were 'brethren peoples' sharing the same territory, and ought to be treated as equals, notwithstanding their cultural differences and traditional hierarchical relationship. Engagement with, and direct influence on, Sami ethnopolitics has continued in Norwegian anthropology up to the present day. However, I shall argue that a peculiar 'homeblindness' – a lack of reflexivity concerning one's own cultural background – which is ultimately caused by the anthropologists' double role as scholars and as citizens, has contributed to this research, as well as that on immigrants, in largely unnoticed ways.

Stages in Anthropological Research on Sami

Modern anthropological research on Norwegian Sami, which has chiefly been undertaken by Norwegian researchers (Robert Paine being one prominent exception), can be divided into three stages equally reflecting the intellectual development of the discipline after the Second World War and the political circumstances impinging on it. A representative work in the first stage, to which Gjessing himself was a diligent contributor, was Vorren and Manker's *Samekulturen* ('The Sami Culture', 1957), a book that went through many reprints and was still on the mandatory reading list for first-year undergraduates in the early 1980s. The book fits into an ethnological discourse where the main objective of the science of culture consists in the classification and description of presumedly clearly bounded cultures. The authors describe patterns of settlement, beliefs, technology (the first hundred pages of the book are devoted to 'material culture' – we had just been taught the Geertzian concept of culture and were mildly disgusted by the idea that culture could be material), social organisation and artistic expressivity. Vorren and Manker's classificatory subdivisions of transhumant Sami, coastal Sami, forest Sami and Skolt Sami (thus named because of their characteristic headdress) are controversial today, both for political reasons and because the categories do not necessarily correspond to sociologically interesting facts; but the most obviously dated part of the book is the short chapter which discusses the Sami as a biological people. The chapters about the coastal and forest Sami have a perceptible element of cultural history since their 'form of culture proper has been covered up quite comprehensively by the cultural evolution of the last centuries in the Sami homeland' (Vorren and Manker 1957: 83). This is, briefly, a work of descriptive ethnography, which takes Romantic notions of cultural purity for granted, and which emphasizes the *uniqueness* of the Sami. It is a work of splendid craftsmanship, and stands squarely in an 'Orientalist' tradition typical of Sami studies since the nineteenth century. Although the authors do discuss questions of minority rights and do not see the impact of modernity as pernicious per se, they confirm a common image of the Sami as noble savages, and their book arguably contributed to strengthening a widespread Norwegian fascination for the simple life of the North, as well as a notion of the Sami as being radically different from other Norwegians. In this, Vorren and Manker's volume was out of sync with the mainstream Anglophone anthropology of the 1950s, which eschewed race and tried to develop a neutral, non-exoticizing language in its ethnographic practice.

At the same time as the newfangled social anthropology, largely an import from the UK, began to phase out the wide-ranging cultural science represented by Gjessing at the Ethnographic Museum, following which Fredrik Barth and his students developed a powerful department of social anthropology in Bergen (see also Eriksen 2008a), there was a shift in focus and emphasis in Sami studies. This second stage in modern Sami studies was defined not only by the shift from a cultural history paradigm to a sociologically oriented social anthropology, but also by the publication of Harald Eidheim's few but influential articles about Sami-Norwegian ethnicity (see Eidheim 1971 for a selection). Eidheim's perspective on ethnicity, which was a clear influence on Barth's (1969) celebrated introduction to *Ethnic Groups and Boundaries* (where Eidheim's chapter has the Goffmanesque title 'When Ethnic Identity Is a Social Stigma'), was initially inspired by symbolic interactionism and the Manchester school (Gluckman, Clyde Mitchell et al.), but was later enriched by Bateson's system theory (Eriksen 2008b). In his string of articles where he saw ethnicity as a relationship, not as a cultural essence, Eidheim was concerned with the 'fashioning of identity' and the phenomenon later known as strategic essentialism, whereby minorities actively overcommunicate and undercommunicate (Goffman's terms again) aspects of their culture, for strategic reasons. Through this approach, the 'essence of Sami culture', hitherto a defining aspect of Saminess, became part of the defined space (cf. Ardener 1989); the cultural needed accounting for rather than accounting for behaviour; it became *explanandum* rather than *explanans*.

In parsimonious, precise prose, Eidheim identified the significant relationships defining the Sami-Norwegian space, and showed how ethnicity could be studied semantically, as processes of signification. Key terms were dichotomisation (contrasting with the other), complementarization (matching with the other), opportunity situation (a term from Barth) and stigma (from Goffman). He showed how particular cultural diacritica became authoritative in early Sami ethnopolitics, and which strategies might be employed in order to achieve symbolic (and consequently political) equity. The focus was now on asymmetrical local power relationships and symbolic relationships, and on 'the management of identity'.

The semantic core in Sami identity, as it is described in these classic articles, consists in language and reindeer. The 'impure' coastal Sami, dealt with in the article on stigma, are depicted here – as in earlier research – as 'the poor cousin'. In Vorren and Manker's book, it is apparent that the coastal Sami have little exotic value, and this also indirectly becomes evident in Eidheim's work, especially if one compares the stigma article with 'Assimilation, Ethnic Incorporation and the Problem of Identity Management' (the concluding essay in Eidheim 1971). They regularly interact with ethnic Norwegians, and few visible diacritica distinguish the groups from one another. Roughly in the same way as the 'ethnically impure' Scandinavian Romani or travellers (*tatere*) have been treated with much less romantic interest than Roma (Gypsies), the 'impure' coastal Sami have, according to narratives of the Second Phase kind, been offered the worst of both worlds: stigma because they are different, but few if any cultural signs to convert into identity capital.

A veritable flood of dissertations, articles, books and lectures, especially emanating from the University of Tromsø (near the traditional Sami areas, thus attracting many Sami students), use Eidheim's work as their analytical foundation. His research perspective has also had a perceptible impact on its object, that is Sami ethnopolitics and ethnic relations to the majority. More recent scholarly work reports on how 'ordinary Sami' actively relate to Eidheim's stigma perspective (Hovland 1996, Thuen 1995). Another highly visible consequence of the Eidheim approach is the recognition, more clearly articulated among Sami than in any other indigenous group I am aware of, that cultural identity is dynamic, relational, flexible and malleable, and that group membership is a question of ascription by self and others, not of cultural traits. In this way, Eidheim's studies have had real-world consequences, many would argue of a liberating kind, in Sápmi. The President of the Sami Parliament from 1997 to 2005, Sven-Roald Nystø, incidentally holds a degree in social anthropology from Tromsø.

A comprehensive standard work summing up this second stage, both in anthropological studies of Sami identity and in the history of Sami ethnopolitics (the two are not always easy to disentangle), is arguably Trond Thuen's *Quest for Equity* (Thuen 1995), although others, including Robert Paine and his *Herds of the Tundra* (1994), also produced important work in the period. Thuen's book demonstrates the growth of cultural reflexivity and political professionalism among Sami from the late 1950s to the early 1990s, a period culminating in the inauguration of the Sami parliament and, one might add to Thuen's account, the official apology to the Sami for Norwegian oppression over the centuries, delivered by King Harald V in 1997.

A third stage in anthropological studies of the Sami may roughly be said to have begun in the early 1990s, a period of transition worldwide – one can mention the end of the Cold War, the coming of the Internet and mobile phones, the beginning of the end of apartheid, the breakup of Yugoslavia and the Rushdie affair – and also, in the far north, marked by the state's recognition of Sami autonomy. This period in Sami research has been equally influenced by the legacy of the Eidheim/Barth school of ethnicity studies, postcolonial theory and that kind of 'deconstructivism light' often referred to as the 'Writing Culture' perspective, where the evocative, rhetorical and creative aspects of anthropological writing are simultaneously examined and openly made a part of the research enterprise.

This phase has been characterised by the increased activity of Sami scholars and by critiques and countercritiques of the concept of culture. Identity has replaced ethnicity as a dominant term, possibly as a result of the increased influence of American anthropology at the expense of the British tradition, leading to an increased focus on psychological and symbolic processes instead of social organisation, which was the unquestioned basis for even Eidheim's ventures into semantics. Vigdis Stordahl's dissertation and book about identity dilemmas in Karasjok (Stordahl 1996) is a central work in this stage (Stordahl being a Sami herself); similarly, Arild Hovland's (1996) comparative study of identity management in Kåfjord and Kautokeino.

In a certain sense, however, this phase may have been initiated by Ivar Bjørklund's *Fjordfolket i Kvænangen* ('The Fjord People of Kvænangen', 1985). Bjørklund discovered that the population of this fjord were 'actually' Sami, but that their Sami identity had been lost – they had forgotten their Sami origins. Kvænangen was probably one of the communities Eidheim had in mind when he wrote, two decades earlier, about coastal hamlets where most of the population had at some stage been Sami, but had gradually become assimilated into an ethnically Norwegian identity.

In the years following Bjørklund's fieldwork, a notable ethnicization of the coastal Sami has taken place. Hitherto, the conventional leftist view among Norwegians associated the Sami 'quest for equity' with the 'authentic' reindeer herders, and there is a clear continuity between early modern Norwegian conservatives and their romantic attitudes towards the authentic savages of the north and, generations later, the children of 1968 and their wish to salvage authentic Sami culture.

The causes of the ethnicization of the 'impure and inauthentic' coastal Sami are at least partly obvious. From the early 1980s, an ideological situation developed, in Norway as elsewhere in the world, where it became possible and sometimes even politically profitable to promote one's interests *qua* ethnic group. Whereas Stordahl (1996) describes the growth of state-sponsored cultural institutions supporting both cultural continuity and careful modernisation in inland Finnmark (the reindeer herding areas), most of Hovland's *Moderne urfolk* ('Modern indigenes', 1996) devoted to the more controversial aspects of the (re-)vitalisation processes in Kåfjord, a coastal area far from the core reindeer herding region. Since very many of the inhabitants of Northern Norway in fact have mixed origins, it is perfectly possible for thousands of North Norwegians to overcommunicate, selectively, parts of their heritage that makes them credible Norwegians, Sami or *kven* (Norwegians of Finnish origin, the third major ethnic group in the area). Thus, Hovland shows, neighbourhoods, circles of friends and even nuclear families risk to be divided in a situation of heightened ethnic awareness and multiculturalist politics. Arriving in a local community in the coastal North some time in the early 2000s, I was met with the self-mocking greeting, 'Welcome to the Yugoslavia of the north'.

Like Eidheim in his working paper *Stages in the Development of Sami Selfhood* (1992), both Stordahl and Hovland describe a condition of reflexive modernity, where the 'natives' have absorbed anthropological jargon and conceptualisations, using terms like ethnic stigma and identity management as well as constructivist and dynamic concepts of culture actively in their identity work. Although both scholars have produced well-researched work of high analytical sophistication, neither of them critically interrogate the strategic essentialism, sometimes tinged with postmodern self-mockery, which gives ethnic identity the pride of place compared with other possible forms of identification.

Whereas the first phase in post-war research on the Sami was chiefly ethnological, the second phase was interactionist and system-theoretical, and the third phase has been characterised by constructivist perspectives on identification and deconstructivist approaches to culture, inspired by recent theoretical developments in Anglophone anthropology. Nonetheless, there are some clear continuities which run through the entire period.

First, the discourse is almost completely devoid of a class perspective, which must be a result of the strongly politicised situation giving priority to ethnic labels. The NSR (*Norske samers riksforbund*, The National Association of Norwegian Sami), supported by most of the anthropologists during the Alta dam controversy around 1980, is led by academics, and has been the most important political vehicle for the reindeer herders and 'authentic Sami culture'.

The competing SLF (*Samenes landsforbund*, The National Sami Caucus) gets much of its support from the coastal Sami, and has been much more oriented towards class questions than the NSR; in practice, the SLF, dominated by social democrats, has often been willing to sacrifice ethnic uniqueness in order to achieve equality (and is, in this respect, more reminiscent of an immigrant minority NGO than of an indigenous movement).

Secondly, exoticism is still perceptible, 30 years after the publication of *Orientalism*. As Hovland (1996) has pointed out, however, this exoticism sometimes appears through self-exoticization, often informed by earlier anthropological studies of themselves.

Thirdly, most remarkably, Norwegianness is scarcely problematised at all in these studies of Norwegian–Sami relationships. From Vorren and Manker to Hovland and Stordahl, one is given to understand that there exists a Norwegian culture with particular traits, to which Sami relate in a variety of ways (ranging from voluntary assimilation to total rejection). The variation in cultural identity strategies among Sami, thus, does not appear to be a result of associating with different versions of Norwegianness but of mixing the 'Norwegian' and the 'Sami' in varying ratios. Briefly, the boundaries remain, even in the most sophisticated accounts of Sami identity work, such as Hovland's discussion of cultural creolization in Finnmark, or Stordahl's descriptions of Sami modernities lodged between a monolithic 'Norwegianness' and a more diverse Sami cultural world. The fact that emic notions and political realities encourage such dichotomies is no excuse – anthropologists have to do better than serve as mouthpieces for their informants if they are to function effectively as critical intellectuals in a public sphere.

Some Anthropological Contributions to Immigrant Research

The second important minority discourse in the Norwegian public sphere in general, and in anthropology in particular, concerns immigrants, refugees and asylum-seekers. In this field, the academic dominance of anthropology has been much less obvious than in Sami research. Both criminologists, sociologists, media researchers and education scholars have produced important contributions to immigrant research. As a result, class and gender have figured more prominently, culture less so, than in research on Sami. I shall nevertheless limit myself here to commenting on a few anthropological contributions to Norwegian immigrant research.

Early anthropological studies of immigration to Norway include, *inter alia*, Grønhaug (1979) and Kramer (1979). Writing at a time when non-Western immigrants were few and recent (total immigrant numbers rose from 20,000 in 1973 to 450,000 in 2008), Reidar Grønhaug explained the internal logic of labour migration from Anatolia to Norway, pointing out how the asymmetrical symbolic power relations between Turks and Norwegians entailed a form of cultural disqualification, in a way not entirely unlike Eidheim's analysis of cultural stigma. Julian Kramer, himself an immigrant from South Africa, showed how the Indians of a middle-sized Norwegian town tried to combine full integration into Norwegian institutions with maintenance of cultural and religious identity. So far, culture had not been politicised to any great extent.

Since these modest beginnings, a great number of anthropological studies of immigrants have been produced. Some of this work has been commissioned by local or state government, but even much of that which is not, strictly speaking, applied research, discusses questions of 'integration' from a point of view virtually indistinguishable from that of the state.

Typical publications from the first period of anthropological engagement with immigrants are Long Litt Woon's edited, interdisciplinary *Fellesskap til besvær?* ('Community of troubles?', 1992), which discusses issues of identification, discrimination and integration; Ottar Brox' *Jeg er ikke rasist, men …* ('I'm not a racist, but …' , 1991), a survey of xenophobic attitudes among ethnic Norwegians; my own *Veien til et mer eksotisk Norge* ('Towards a more exotic Norway, Eriksen 1991), a critical essay on the role of cultural relativism in majority–minority relations; and a sprinkling of others with varying, but perceptible public impact. The debate, both inside and outside of anthropology, focused at the time on racism and discrimination on the one hand, and problems of integration on the other. By the mid-1990s, as new groups of immigrants (refugees mostly) entered the country, public and academic interest in the issues grew, and disagreements among the anthropologists became apparent. Increasingly, an impatient public demanded of the immigrants that they 'integrate' as soon as possible; the benign 'colourful community' rhetoric of the 1980s was suddenly condemned as being 'politically correct', and issues to do with enforced marriages and Islam came to the fore. Unni Wikan wrote *Mot en ny norsk underklasse?* ('Towards a new Norwegian underclass?', 1995), which in no small degree implied that patriarchal ideologies among immigrants (especially Muslims) were instrumental in hindering not only the freedom of minority women but also the full integration (participation? assimilation?) of immigrants in Norwegian society. Wikan was duly criticised, by colleagues and others, for not problematizing, or even discussing, the 'Norwegian culture', but her book had a perceptible impact on the public discourse and official policy over the ensuing years.

The same period saw the publication of a diverse range of academic or popularised books by anthropologists on minority issues, including Øivind Fuglerud's erudite and thorough book on long-distance nationalism among Tamils (Fuglerud 1999), Mary Bente Bringslid's study of refugees in a small Western Norwegian community (Bringslid 1996), Torunn Arntsen Sørheim's work on health and disease among Pakistani-Norwegians (Sørheim 2001) and Inger-Lise Lien's book on racist attitudes among Norwegians and Pakistani (Lien 1996). Several of these books, especially those by Wikan and Lien, were subject to controversy in the press and in seminar rooms, as they voiced critical views towards immigrants and 'their culture'. In an earlier article, Lien (1991) had raised critical questions concerning the normative aspects of immigrant research, asking rhetorically if it was the duty of the anthropologist to defend practices and attitudes among 'their people' even if they were objectionable. One typical answer to this question would be that the work of the anthropologist consists in translating and analysing social and cultural contexts, not to grade them on a moral scale. However, in the area of immigrant research, just as in Sami research, normative questions seem to be unavoidable; the boundary between the political and the academic is chronically thin, slippery and permeable, and the work of anthropologists becomes public by default. As Aud Talle at the University of Oslo discovered in the early 2000s after having been lampooned as a dangerous relativist in the largest newspaper in the country, doing research on female circumcision among Maasai or Somali is unproblematic as far as the wider public is concerned, but identical research on Somali refugees in Norway is fraught with moral implications.

Of the many later publications on minority issues, Marianne Gullestad's *Det norske sett med nye øyne* ('Norwegianness in a new key', Gullestad 2002) deserves special mention. This book explores the cultural categories and semantics prevalent in the majority, showing how discourse about minorities and immigrants is based on tacit assumptions of cultural superiority and the 'backwardness' of immigrants. Drawing on postcolonial theory rather than the Barth-Eidheim ethnicity perspective, Gullestad's monograph marked, in many ways, a new start.

Inger-Lise Lien's view, in her important 1991 article, was that a particular political agenda had informed and contributed to shaping research, with the result that academic work on minority issues became partial and partisan. In fact, anthropologists have enjoyed direct influence on Norwegian integration policy, not least Lien herself, for years an active member of the Labour party, and Wikan, whose advice has been sought by several political parties. I was myself a board member of an anti-racist NGO, *Antirasistisk Senter*, in the 1990s.

In order to assess the relationship between Norwegian anthropological research on minority–majority relations 'at home' and the public sphere, it is necessary first to describe briefly the role of minorities in mainstream political discourse.

Immigrants and Sami in Norwegian Politics of Culture

In general, Sami and immigrant organisations have chosen different strategies in their quest for recognition and equity in Norway. Whereas the Sami organisations (notably the NSR) emphasized cultural uniqueness, history and tradition, immigrant organisations have tended to emphasize equality, giving priority to the struggle against discrimination. With a few exceptions to do with language and religion, their objective has been to achieve formal equality in the labour and housing markets, in the educational institutions and so on. Whereas the Sami represent the Fourth World, immigrants represent the Third World; in academic discourse, the former are an indigenous population, while the latter represent a globalised proletariat. Whereas the Sami lay claim to a unique culture under siege from the modern state, immigrants cannot do so, both because they have their origins in many different countries, and because their culture appears to be perfectly safe and sound in their home country. As a student once wrote, in an exam paper, 'Why should one protect the culture of 150 Indians in "Rivertown" [Kramer's pseudonym], when there are several hundred million Indians in India anyway?'

In mainstream Norwegian politics, views and policies on Sami and on immigrants/immigration have not corresponded in a simple way to the left–right continuum. The left have by and large been pro-immigrant, but have been – and are – divided on multiculturalism, the limits of tolerance and issues to do with religion and women's rights. Regarding the Sami, the attitudes on the left have also been ambivalent, split between a wish to offer equality and full integration into the modern state and the politics of recognition, which would also entail the preservation of Sami culture. These disagreements, incidentally, mirror the dilemmas of liberals and leftists in many countries these days.

The dominant Labour party has by and large been concerned with equality in both contexts, while the Conservative party has tried to define cultural and religious identity as a private matter. Political debates pitting cultural rights against equality have continuously caused controversy both within and between political parties. In 1997, the Finnmark section of the Socialist Left party (SV) was split, and the local party organisation in Karasjok (a main inland Sami town) disbanded itself, following a statement by the top candidate on the Parliamentary list of the party, where he went against the idea that rights to land and water should follow ethnic lines (an important issue for Sami organisations). His argument was that anyone who lived in Finnmark should have the same rights regardless of ethnic identity.

As a minority group with special rights, the Sami nevertheless have much more credibility in the wider public sphere than do the immigrants, and they have a special legal status as an indigenous group.

Anthropologists position themselves explicitly and implicitly in this political landscape. In spite of the considerable differences between the Oslo region (where most of the immigrants live) and Finnmark regarding minority issues, it is possible to identify some commonalities. In 1996, the Pakistani-Norwegian intellectual Naushad Ali Qureshi wrote a lengthy newspaper article where he accused the social anthropologists of having drifted from an exoticizing to a condemning attitude towards minorities. Both attitudes demarcate sharp boundaries between 'us' and 'them', and immigrants are stereotyped and objectified, regardless of whether the gaze of the researcher is admiring or disapproving (Qureshi 1996). In particular, Qureshi targets Wikan (1995), but his article is a general critique of culturalism in social research: through emphasising cultural differences and/or ethnic boundaries, one contributes to strengthening them. Moreover – and this may be the largest problem in Norwegian minority research 'at home' – the *Norwegian* side of the 'boundary' is rarely problematised, but instead stereotyped or neglected (but see Gullestad 2002, 2006). Norway is depicted, in research on immigrants (and one might add, on the Sami), either as a monolithic, liberal society where universalist morality, love marriages and human rights predominate, or as an ethnonationalistic, xenophobic society with little tolerance for cultural diversity.

It must be kept in mind that for many years, academic scholarship on Norwegianness ignored minority issues. Tellingly, the most authoritative collective work on Norwegian identity from the 1980s, Arne Martin Klausen's edited volume *Den norske væremåten* ('The Norwegian way of being', 1984), contains excellent analyses of cultural styles, the rural–urban divide, gender and nature worship, but just one chapter on minorities (by the aforementioned Julian Kramer), and minorities were absent from the analyses of mainstream Norwegian society. Minorities were also conspicuously absent from the work of Marianne Gullestad, the most important anthropologist writing about Norwegians from the mid-1980s until her death in 2008, before she turned to this topic in the late 1990s, which led to the significant (and controversial) 2002 book (see Gullestad 2006). When minorities were finally brought into the analysis of mainstream Norwegian society, it happened largely under the aegis of the Eidheim–Barth ethnicity paradigm.

Conclusions

An ethnicizing framework for engagement with social and cultural phenomena has its costs, whether it is used by politicians or by researchers. An example could be the predicaments inherent in the wide-ranging edited volume *Becoming Visible* (Brantenberg, Hansen and Minde 1995), which offers a representative sample of the discourse on the Sami. The contributors are academics, activists, high-ranking bureaucrats, politicians and artists. The starting point of the book, shared by nearly all the contributors, is the injustice committed against the world's indigenous peoples for centuries, and it also becomes apparent how many such groups, over the last decades, have made progress regarding recognition for their language, customs and land rights. Five basic predicaments are apparent in the book, all of them indirectly relevant for immigrants as well and, for that matter, recognizable in similar research elsewhere in the world.

1. Indigenous peoples risk building an opinion based on the premise that they are 'threatened by extinction' in the same way as whales and pandas. In this case, they risk being accepted as Sami on the condition that they behave like Sami (whatever that entails). Immigrant minorities have nothing to gain from such a rhetoric – on the contrary, their 'cultural impurity' signifies their lesser value. Similarly, the very many Sami who cannot credibly pose as 'authentic' are placed in a vulnerable and precarious situation.

2. The right to a cultural identity may become a straitjacket for individuals who would prefer not to have one. The implicit (and sometimes explicit) message is that a rooted identity is an unquestionable asset. Here, political debate and actual policy on immi-

grants take a different route, and the second generation is virtually encouraged (by politicians and commentators, but also by many academics) to distance itself from the parents' culture.

3. When ethnic membership is made the basis for rights, groups or individuals who cannot lay claim to an ethnic identity are neglected. Thus, the social exclusion of people with no particular ethnic identity – the poor of São Paolo, unemployed people in Oslo – may go unmarked.

4. The emphasis on history (and, not least, prehistory) in indigenous politics makes it difficult for these groups to make a common cause with other ethnic minorities. In Norway, there has scarcely been any collaboration between Sami and immigrants.

5. The relationship between equality and complementarity is unclear in the indigenous discourse. Rights, universal or cultural as the case might be, are claimed situationally, depending on the opportunity situation.

Faced with these dilemmas, anthropological research and public interventions, rather than complementing and critically interrogating identity politics in the public sphere, has tended to reproduce its categories. This voluminous body of research is, in general (there are exceptions), fraught with the following problems:

1. With the exception of 'native' researchers such as Anh Nga Longva (who has written about Vietnamese in Norway) and Vigdis Stordahl, very few have learnt the languages in question well. This is nothing short of a professional scandal, considering the centrality of the Malinowskian emphasis on language learning in Norwegian anthropology when fieldwork takes place abroad.

2. Norwegianness is scarcely problematised (except in Gullestad's aforementioned, recent work). It is either taken for granted, or it remains unmentioned. Thus, the Norwegian obsession with gender equality, for example, becomes an implicit premise for research on, for example, gender roles in the Pakistani-Norwegian family, rather than empirical data to be analysed in its own right. As a result, scholars more or less unwittingly tend to adopt problem formulations originally framed within their own cultural value system. This in turn hampers their ability to ask critical questions to the framing of the issues in the dominant public dis-

course. Incidentally, this form of 'homeblindness' is not unknown in Anglophone anthropology either, where great pains are often taken to describe fine nuances in the local cultures under study, which are then cursorily contrasted with something called 'Western culture'.

3. There is a tendency to adopt uncritically the classic ethnicity paradigm (which was, in its time, an important advance over earlier models), according to which the social universe is constituted of ethnic groups and boundaries, rather than, for example, kinds of relationship. The dynamic (and suitably fuzzy) concept of culture which has predominated in recent years (in what I have labelled the third phase in Sami studies) has done little to change this approach, which conceals non-ethnic social phenomena and may ultimately lead to reductionist ethnographies.

4. The dominant analytical framing of cultural difference is more indebted to Norwegian debates about culture than to anthropological research on cultural differences. This has made Norwegian research on ethnicity 'at home' more provincial than necessary.

My intention with this brief, but critical exploration of Norwegian anthropology on minorities 'at home' has been to show the powerful interrelationship between domestic politics and anthropology at home, rendering public anthropology necessary but also immensely difficult. I have also tried to identify the dangers of not only methodological but also moral homeblindness. The scholar's gaze, even when critical of government policy and hegemonic ideologies, is shaped by the scholar's embroilment with domestic affairs, and risks merely reproducing or mechanically negating a hegemonic discourse, rather than establishing an independent approach growing out of professional concerns. One inevitable conclusion is that we Norwegian anthropologists should extend an open invitation to foreign anthropologists to do research on our society and participate in public debates about it.

Similar problems are likely to occur elsewhere, and they do in countries where anthropologists carry out research 'at home'. What is gained in political influence may be lost in academic relevance, unless anthropologists in their public interventions are more self-conscious about their own role and professional duties as purveyors of the gaze from afar. Anthropologists working at home could, and should in my view, draw more actively on anthropological perspectives developed in other empirical settings. This would enable them to achieve the analytical distance necessary in order to ask questions growing out of the academic discourse rather than domestic political concerns. Since one of anthropology's tasks, seen in a wider intellectual context, consists in asking the unexpected, but illuminating question, and that question might well first have been raised in South Africa or Melanesia. Through such an act of liberation from domestic public discourse, anthropological interventions might become both intellectually more stimulating and, perhaps paradoxically, more relevant politically.

References

Ardener, E. (1989), 'Social Anthropology and Population', in *The Voice of Prophecy and Other Essays,* (ed.) M. Chapman (Oxford: Blackwell), 109–127.

Barth, F. (ed.) (1969), *Ethnic Groups and Boundaries: The Social Organization of Culture Difference.* (Bergen: Univertsitetsforlaget, Scandinavian University Books).

Bjørklund, I. (1985), *Fjordfolket i Kvænangen* (Oslo: Scandinavian University Press).

Bouquet, M. (1996), *Bringing It All Back Home … To the Oslo University Ethnographic Museum* (Oslo: Scandinavian University Press).

Brantenberg, T., J. Hansen and H. Minde, (eds) (1995), *Becoming Visible: Indigenous Politics and Self-government.* Proceedings of the Conference on Indigenous Politics and Self-Government, 8–10 November 1993 (Tromsø: Universitetet i Tromsø).

Bringslid, M. B. (1996), 'Bygda og den framande: Ein studie av det lokales de- og rekontekstualisering i ei vestnorsk bygd'. Dr polit. dissertation, University of Bergen.

Brox, O. (1991), *Jeg er ikke rasist, men …* (Oslo: Gyldendal).

Eidheim, F. (1992), *Sett nordfra* (Oslo: Scandinavian University Press).

Eidheim, H. (1971), *Aspects of the Lappish Minority Situation* (Oslo: Scandinavian University Press).

——— (1992), *Stages in the Development of Sami Selfhood.* Working paper no. 7 (Oslo: Institutt for sosialantropologi).

Eriksen, T. H. (1991), *Veien til et mer eksotisk Norge* (Oslo: Ad Notam).

——— (2008a), 'The Otherness of Norwegian Anthropology', in *Other People's Anthropologies*, (ed.) A. Boskovic (Oxford: Berghahn), 169–185.

——— (2008b), 'Interview with Harald Eidheim'. *Norsk antropologisk tidsskrift* 19, nos. 2–3: 177–188.

Fuglerud, Ø. (1999), *Life on the Outside: The Tamil Diaspora and Long-distance Nationalism* (London: Pluto).

Grønhaug, R. (ed.) (1979), *Migrasjon, utvikling og minoriteter* (Oslo: Scandinavian University Press).

Gullestad, M. (2002), *Det norske sett med nye øyne* (Oslo: Scandinavian University Press).

——— (2006), *Plausible Prejudice: Everyday Experiences and Social Images of Nation, Culture and Race* (Oslo: Scandinavian University Press).

Hovland, A. (1996), *Moderne urfolk. Samisk ungdom i bevegelse* (Oslo: Cappelen Akademisk Forlag).

Klausen, A. M. (ed.) (1984), *Den norske væremåten* (Oslo: Cappelen).

Kramer, J. (1979), 'Indiske innvandrere i en norsk', in *Migrasjon, utvikling og minoriteter*, (ed.) I. R. Grønhaug (Oslo: Scandinavian University Press).

Lien, I. L. (1991), 'En god forsker eller et godt menneske?', *Nytt norsk tidsskrift* 8, no. 2: 177–185.

——— (1996), *Ordet som stempler djevlene: Holdninger blant pakistanere og nordmenn* (Oslo: Aventura).

Long Litt Woon (ed.) (1992), *Fellesskap til besvær? Aspekter ved nyere innvandring til Norge* (Oslo: Scandinavian University Press).

Paine, R. (1994), *Herds of the Tundra: A Portrait of Saami Reindeer Pastoralism* (Washington DC: Smithsonian Institution Press).

Qureshi, N. A. (1996), 'Det står menneskesyn på spill, men hvilket?' *Aftenposten*, 18 May.

Sørheim, T. A. (2001), *Kultur og kommunikasjon: Familier med pakistansk bakgrunn i møte med helsevesenet* (Oslo: Gyldendal).

Stordahl, V. (1996), *Same i den moderne verden: Endring og kontinuitet i et samisk lokalsamfunn* (Karasjok: Davvi Girji).

Thuen, T. (1995), *Quest for Equity. Norway and the Saami Challenge* (St John's: ISER).

Vorren, Ø. and Manker, E. (1957), *Samekulturen* (Tromsø: Tromsø Museum).

Wikan, U. (1995), *Mot en ny norsk underklasse: Innvandrere, kultur og integrasjon* (Oslo: Gyldendal).

Dow Chemical's Knowledge Factories
Action Anthropology against Michigan's Company Town Culture

Brian McKenna

'Growth [is] the opiate we're all hooked on ...'
(Frank Popoff, former CEO of DOW Chemical; in Brandt 1997: 575)

'Growth for whom?'
(in *Dying for Growth, Global Inequality and the Health of the Poor,*
Kim 2000)

When the enterprising Herbert Dow was rummaging in his Midland Michigan shed in the 1890s, few locals knew what the Ohio man was up to. Dow was in fact digging a deep water well to mine the salty brine – from an ancient underwater sea beneath the city – to make bromine. He was applying the knowledge he had mastered at Ohio's Case School of Applied Science to make a chemical – potassium bromide – that he would market to pharmaceutical companies for use as a sedative and stomach soother. The 'chemical genius' Herbert Dow had partnered with the 'money men' from Ohio to finance their obsessive quest to make cash from chemicals (Whitehead 1968: 1–2).

Midland locals were not impressed. As reported in Don Whitehead's, *The Dow Story* (1968), 'In 1903 Midland residents threatened to sue Dow Chemical because of smelly gases', which they claimed induced vomiting (Whitehead 1968: 57). Herbert Dow 'hooted down' the protests as he would time and again after explosions, chemicals and pollution seeped from his plants, disturbing civic life (ibid.). But hooting down the locals over environmental contamination could not work forever. And, in fact, Dow's family and his executive staff lived in Midland too and sought its pleasures, what few there were in a moonscaped place made barren after the nineteenth-century logging craze. Dow money flowed into the village and soon it seemed like every civic and cultural arena had the Dow name attached to it, from the library and gardens to the Museum of Science and Art and historical museum (Whitehead 1968: 277). Midland became a company town and the locals, dependent on the money and grateful for Dow's largess, were quieted.

A century later Dow's reach as a creator of pollution extends around the globe. On 3 December 1984, just after midnight, 40 tons of poisonous substances leaked from Union Carbide's pesticide plant in Bhopal, central India. A huge yellow cloud exposed half a million people to the gases, which hung over the city for hours. It remains the worst industrial accident of all time. Although the numbers are still in dispute there were over 3,000 deaths and 100,000 injuries in the first few days and several thousand additional claims of injuries or deaths to date (Doyle 2004: 420). In 2001 Michigan's Dow Chemical purchased Union Carbide, assuming the historic weight of its outstanding liabilities to the people of Bhopal. The international community shifted its attention to Dow Chemical for social justice. But in Michigan itself, few citizens are aware of any relationship between Dow and Bhopal. How does this happen, especially in a culture that prides itself on freedom of speech and academic freedom?

I discovered the Bhopal connection in 2002 while updating my knowledge on the tragedy for a course I was teaching at Michigan State University as an adjunct professor. The class was called 'Global Diversity and Interdependence'. I was surprised at the news because Dow's International headquarters in Midland is just 60 miles from MSU. After discussing the Dow–Bhopal connection with my class of 250 students, I was approached, after class, by an irate student who expressed anger at my mentioning the issue. A very close relative of hers, she told me, was the CEO of Dow Chemical. At the time MSU's president was Peter McPherson, a close friend of Vice President Dick Cheney. The former head of the U.S. Agency for International Development, McPherson later took a leave of absence from MSU, in 2003, to serve in Iraq for President Bush. After my conversation with the student, I consulted with my friend Dave Dempsey, the Policy Director of the Michigan Environmental Council, for advice. He suggested that I stage a debate. The subsequent debate, 'Is Dow Chemical a Good Corporate Citizen?' was well received and turned a potential problem into a good pedagogical moment.

Public Anthropology, Civic Engagement and Activism: The Local as Exotic

In fact, the question of Dow's so called 'corporate citizen' status is an oxymoron. Dow's primary interest is capital accumulation. Democracy and citizenship education are threats to its enterprise, as we shall see. Subsequent to the 2002 classroom debate, I published nearly all of what follows as a Michigan journalist. This included the Ann Arbor Ecology Center's *From the Ground Up* (2004a) and Michigan's *Lansing City Pulse* newspaper (2002, 2004b), where I was a weekly columnist. This work was reproduced or updated in several outlets including *CounterPunch* (2005, 2008a, 2008b, 2008c) a daily Internet newsletter which receives over half a million views per month, as well as *Corporate Watch, Bhopal.Net,* and *CommonDreams*. It was also featured in the American Anthropology Association's series *Pulse of the Planet* in November 2008. This work is part of a larger project in which I seek to diagnose a new company town culture, including the growing corporatization of the university and media, in neoliberal America. It is also part of another project to improve the theory and practice of public pedagogy in anthropology (McKenna 2009).

My Dow–MSU work is a form of what anthropologist Charles Hale calls *Engaging Contradictions* (Hale 2008) as his book is titled. A few months after learning about the Dow–Bhopal connection, for example, I found another significant contradiction. In the Spring of 2002, Dow co-sponsored a seminar series at MSU's Detroit College of Law called 'Creating Sustainable Cities in the 21st Century'. On 19 March the talk was titled 'Abandonment of the Cities'. I noted to myself that there was no mention that day of the irony that Dow Chemical had abandoned the city of Bhopal. Moreover, there were no protests even though MSU had a nationally renowned campus sustainability programme. So, a few days later I wrote about it in my weekly environmental column as a local journalist (McKenna 2002). This was one of 33 weekly columns I wrote during that period. Soon I was asked by an MSU social scientist, who had influence over my adjunct employment, to stop writing about MSU after s/he received a phone call from MSU administration. I chose to continue writing since I considered it important social science.

Jennifer Washburn describes the stakes tellingly in her important work, *University, Inc., The Corporate Corruption of American Higher Education* (2005), 'As universities have become commercial entities, the space to perform research that is critical of industry or that challenges conventional market ideology – research on environmental pollution, poverty alleviation, occupational health hazards – has gradually diminished, as has the willingness of universities to defend professions whose findings conflict with the interests of their corporate sponsors' (Washburn 2005: 227). She asks, 'Will universities stand up for academic freedom in these situations, or will they bow to commercial pressure out of fear of alienating donors?' and concludes 'Too often of late, it has been the latter.' (ibid.). And yet, without publicly engaged activist anthropology I would never have written this very article before you. As Hale correctly notes, 'Activism is not just a matter of publicity or reaching broader publics with a message from social science. It is a way of *doing social science* [emphasis mine], often in collaboration with non-social scientists. … [it] is part of the process of forming, testing, and improving knowledge' (Hale 2008: xvii).

It is not just corporate donors and disciplinary norms that can constrain free inquiry, but for some universities, it is foreign governments. This is of increasing importance in Great Britain. In March 2009 Great Britain's Centre for Social Coherence released a groundbreaking report *A Degree of Influence: The funding of strategically important subjects in UK universities* (Simcox 2009) that detailed how Arabic and Islamic countries are contributing large sums – often anonymously – in strategic curricular areas. It shows how universities are being used as diplomatic arms of those countries. With entire departments dependent on foreign contributions, a climate of censorship and self-censorship is fostered: 'universities have insufficient safeguards in place to prevent donations affecting the way universities are run. There is clear evidence that, at some universities, the choice of teaching materials, the subject areas, the degrees offered, the recruitment of staff, the composition of advisory boards and even the selection of students are now subject to influence from donors' (Simcox 2009: 12–13).

PhDs and the Magical Circle of Knowledge

One might think that a large group of highly educated PhDs is sufficient to protect critical inquiry. Midland, Michigan 'has more PhDs per square acre than you'll find most anywhere else', Don Whitehead reported in *The Dow Story* 40 years ago (1968: 276). That is just as true today. But all that brainpower has not translated into much critical intervention against Dow's practices and policies in Midland, where citizens live under the conditions of a company town. Many are beholden to Dow for their livelihoods, and everyone's property values are held hostage to the idea that dioxin – one of the most dangerous substances known to man – is not really harmful and the contamination of their yards, parks, playgrounds and water is really not that significant. Whitehead provides insight into this mindset: 'Those who seek anonymity after working hours and who wish to build a wall between their business lives and their private lives find the small town a very difficult place. Such walls are not easy to build in a small town. The town's life is not different from the life of the company. One impinges on the other in many ways' (Whitehead 1968: 10).

One might expect Michigan's universities – located safely outside Midland's geographical sphere of influence – to be more independent and critical of Dow Chemical. But as Stanley Aronowitz makes clear in *The Knowledge Factory, Dismantling the Corporate University and Creating True Higher Learning* (2000), the current business craze in academia has blurred the distinctions between training, education and learning. As educational theorist Henry Giroux pointed out in an interview, 'educators need to take seriously the importance of defending higher education as an institution of civic culture whose purpose is to educate students for active and critical citizenship … markets don't reward moral behaviour' (Giroux, personal communication) And markets are what Dow is all about.

There is a growing scholarship on this crisis. In the book *Campus, Inc.* (White 2000), for example, 39 contributors explored topics including the myth of the liberal campus, organizing advice for campus combatants, and rethinking academic culture. One necessary form of academic rethinking concerns the very content and structure of disciplinary knowledge itself: specialization. Academics need to understand better the forms of social control that have transformed them into specialists writing for a small, narrow audience (Jacoby 1987). Bledstein's formulation of the 'magical circle of scientific knowledge' (1976: 90), has characterized academics as self-conscious members of an exclusive club in which members believe that only the few specialized by training and indoctrination are privileged to enter. Academics configure social problems in accordance with the specialized rituals of their specific disciplines, he said. For Bledstein (1976), these magical circles of specialized expertise are the basis for both the professions' contribution to society and for the avoidance of society's problems. The result was a fragmentary effort whereby any holistic notion does not work very well. It is ironic that anthropology, the alleged science of holism, too often tends to fall under this academic hegemony.

A holistic engagement is a civic engagement. It is by its nature critical. Therefore it comes with risks. And yet, this holistic, interdisciplinary engagement – as journalists or public writers – is all the more important at a time when the journalistic profession has significantly been scaled back and chilled under severe corporate pressure, undermining critical public culture (Giroux 2007). Anthropologist Thomas Eriksen (2006) agrees. He argues for an 'engaged anthropology' where anthropologists step out of their academic cocoon to embrace the wider public. '[Anthropology's] lack of visibility is an embarrassment and a challenge' (Eriksen 2006: ix). Eriksen argued that anthropology must write in a popular vein to make sense of peoples' lives to the people in their own communities. Anthropologists can alternately use their intellectual resources to make the familiar exotic or the exotic familiar in their own communities. The corporation as a cultural form is tailor-made for this treatment. It is perhaps the most animistic entity known to man. It is treated constitutionally as a living breathing human being. Anthropologists need not travel to all four corners of the globe in search of the exotic: it is right before their eyes 'at home'.

On the Dow Dole

Dow has invested millions into Michigan State University. For example, it gave US$5 million to build the Dow Institute for Materials Research, a 46,000-square-foot addition to the east wing of MSU's Engineering Building, in 1996. In March 2000, Dow Chemical made a biotech deal with Michigan State University in which it would pay MSU about US$4 million over several years. The project focuses on plant oils that might be used in areas like low-cholesterol cooking oil and plastics (McKenna 2004a). Dow hopes new patents will arise to improve its bottom line. Tim Martin, a journalist with the *Lansing State Journal,* spoke with Bob Huggett, MSU's vice president of research and graduate studies about corporate influence, in his 17 April 2000 article, *MSU Weighs Rewards, Risks of Research* (Martin 2000). Martin pointed out that 'critics worry that universities can get too cozy with corporations that sponsor their research, fearing that competition for money could lead schools like MSU to do research that does not help the public, or worse, skew research test results in favor of those paying the bills' (Martin 2000: B1). Martin reported that MSU officials said the source of money does not influence their quest for truth. 'Are we selling our soul to the devil by taking industrial money? I don't think so, [Huggett told Martin] … Corporations have relied more on universities to help their research efforts in the past decade … I don't think that's a problem, as long as we protect what the university stands for – the free and open dissemination of data' (Martin 2000: B4).

But the free and open dissemination of *data* (which is not always so easily accessible), while very important, is not the same as a rigorous search for the truth, or the free and open dissemination of *ideas*, a supposed hallmark of universities. Does education produced for the market undermine education produced for a critical citizenry? Befitting its interdisciplinary goals, does the university present a complete portrait of Dow to all its students? Is Dow a good corporate 'citizen' deserving of an association with a university?

The Long Shadow of Dow

In November 2003, Steve Meador completed a 90-minute documentary titled, 'The Long Shadow' – a critical investigation of Dow's dioxin dealings with Michigan's state government – alone and on a shoestring budget, as a master's project for his environmental journalism degree. Meanwhile, just down the hall from the environmental journalism offices at MSU's Communication Arts Building, a fledgling undergraduate Public Relations specialization is just getting off the ground. It is in honour of E. N. Brandt, whose 1997 book, *Growth Company, Dow Chemical's First Century*, largely sang the praises of 'one of the wonders of the modern business world' (Brandt: 2000: xii). The endowed E. N. Brandt chair was the result of a US$1.3 million gift to MSU from the Carl Gerstacker Foundation in 2000. And who is Carl Gerstacker? Most MSU faculty do not know. He is the former CEO of Dow Chemical. I will address Meador's film first and later return to Brandt.

Meador's film documented what happened after Michigan Governor Engler learned, in 2001, that dioxin levels in the Tittabwassee River floodplain, downstream from Midland's Dow Chemical were found at over 7,000 parts per trillion (80 times Michigan's cleanup standards) near parks and residential areas. They did not bother to tell anyone. Finally, two citizen groups, the Lone Tree Council and the Michigan Environmental Council filed a Freedom of Information Act request to get the data, alerted by conscientious Michigan Department of Environmental Quality (MDEQ) insiders. In January 2002 the FOIA revealed that MDEQ Director Russ Harding had blocked further soil testing and was suppressing a state health assessment that called for aggressive state action. Later the Engler administration secretly tried to work out a 'sweetheart deal' with Dow to raise the clean-up level of dioxin to 831 parts per trillion, thus circumventing clean-up of the dioxin in most areas. A judge later threw this out.

In an effort to appeal to the widest audience, the documentary carefully explained all sides of the controversy. It is neutral in tone, unsensational and almost legalistic in its style. For example, Meador politely interviewed Harding in the film. The film also interviewed Kathy Henry, one of the floodplain residents who lives downstream from Dow's Midland factories. She was advised by the MDEQ to remove her clothing the moment she enters the house after mowing her lawn. Henry looks out at her property as a wasteland. Verifying this, in November 2004, the state of Michigan issued a game consumption advisory for the Tittabawassee river floodplain because of Dow's dioxin. Turkeys and deer are now considered potentially toxic. This was only the second time in Michigan history that such a warning was made (McKenna 2004a).

Two Films and Two Terrorisms: Public or Private TV?

'Unfortunately, The Long Shadow was never shown on Michigan PBS', said Meador in an interview (McKenna 2005: 1). Meador sent a rough cut to four stations – WCMU (Mt Pleasant), WFUM at the University of Michigan (Flint), WTVS (Detroit), and WKAR at Michigan State University (East Lansing) in December 2003. 'All of these stations had broadcast a previous documentary of mine entitled "A May to Remember" about the Bath School bombing of 1927. Strangely, all of the stations were completely unresponsive to "The Long Shadow" (i.e., phone calls and e-mails not returned)' (McKenna 2005: 2). Meador said the film's merits have been recognized by environmental reporters from the Bay City Times (Jeff Kart) and Detroit Free Press (Hugh McDiarmid). '"The affected residents in the floodplain also had very nice things to say about it," he added. "I'm not sure why the PBS stations didn't bite. A number of people have suggested that the stations shied away because they are underwritten by Dow, and I think that is a possibility"' (McKenna 2005: 2).

When the focus is on a single demented terrorist the public airwaves are available, but when the gaze turns to a transnational guilty of poisoning vast swaths of mid-Michigan with dioxin – which the Environmental Protection Agency classifies as a highly toxic persistent organochlorine that causes cancer – that's a different story, especially when the public airwaves are partly underwritten by the trans-national corporation. In fact, Dow Chemical is associated with a world historic form of industrial terrorism. Given the death counts, the prolonged agony and the persistent callous treatment of its victims, the Union Carbide/Dow Chemical disaster is far worse than the September 11th tragedy. Yet it is invisible in Michigan.

Dow's Version of History

Dow is a big funder to universities that house three of these public television stations. For example, WCMU is at Central Michigan University, 30 miles from Midland. In 1978 Dow's President withdrew money from CMU after Jane Fonda spoke there on economic democracy. '[It] will not be resumed until we are convinced our dollars are not expended in supporting those who would destroy us' (Brandt 1997: 527). CMU got the message. It's new 'Herbert H. and Grace A. Dow College of Health Professions' touts Dow even though DOW only gave US$5 million, while MI taxpayers gave US$37.5 million. Brandt approvingly quoted columnist George Will on Dow Chemical's decision at the time: '"Capitalism inevitably nourishes a hostile class," said Will. "American business has been generous with gifts to universities … but too indiscriminate. Dow has given the business community a timely sample of appropriate discrimination"' (Brandt 1997: 527).

Brandt's thick volume represented Dow's view of the world. Predictably, it dismissed dioxin's real-life dangers, citing study after study apparently disproving a health problem. Brandt tells the story of a '60 Minutes' crew who arrived in Midland, soon after Times Beach, Missouri was evacuated for dioxin pollution in 1982, expecting Midland to be the next town evacuated because of dioxin contamination (Brandt 1997).

'They came at the busiest weekend of the year,' Brandt quotes a Dow official as saying, 'everybody's laughing and having a big time at the art fair, and the antique show you have to see to believe … They're having trouble finding beleaguered folks. To make a long story short, with the exception of a few environmentalists from a local organization, they gave up. That story just went away because they could not find any substance for their story line' (Brandt 1997: 365–366). This 649-page treatise spent a great deal of time defending Dow against various interlocutors. In a chapter called 'Flower Children' Brandt dismissed all the 'napalm hubbub' (Brandt 1997: 362) created by Vietnam War activists, claiming that napalm was, according to secretary of defence McNamara, of little consequence to civilians and was 'a great service for the armed forces' (Brandt 1997: 357).

Brandt defended Dow against the 1941 charge by the U.S. Justice Department that Dow conspired with the Nazi's I.F. Farben to hold down magnesium production in the United States in the pre-war era (Dow later pleaded *nolo contendere*), but failed to mention Dow's 1951 hiring of Otto Ambros, the Nazi war criminal convicted at Nuremberg for slavery and mass murder in the killing of thousands of Jews with poison gas (well detailed in the excellent 1991 book, 'Secret Agenda', by Linda Hunt). Brandt informed us that Dow was the first company to receive a phone call from Pinochet's military in 1973 soon after his forces assassinated democratically elected Chilean President Salvador Allende, toppling his government, asking Dow to come back, which Dow 'readily accepted' (a Dow official saluting the economic 'miracle' of Pinochet) (Brandt 1997: 453). But Brandt's book never mentions the thousands tortured and 3,000 killed during Pinochet's brutal dictatorship.

Tapping the Brain Bank

Dow Chemical has established deep-seated connections to everything from biotechnology, engineering and military research, to public health, public relations and journalism. In so doing, Dow has constructed a benevolent corporate image while mining expertise and reaping patent rewards. In recent years Dow and its offshoots (like the Gerstacker Foundation) have contributed more than US$10 million in direct contributions to the University of Michigan, including US$5 million in 2000 to fund a new College of Engineering laboratory; US$2.5 million in 2000 for the Dow Chemical Company Professor of Sustainable Science, Technology, and Commerce; and US$1.2 million to the U-M School of Public Health in 1996 for a Dow professorship focusing on the health effects, risks and benefits of chemicals in the environment. The Dow Chair at Saginaw Valley State University is chemistry Professor David H. Swenson. In a 9 April 2002 article in the *Saginaw News* he said that when environmental groups clash with alleged polluters, the claims of both groups often are suspect. In a follow-up interview Swenson said that 'the [dioxin] data is fuzzy and unclear … we know it's [damaging] to mice [at given levels] but it's hard to see if that translates directly into humans'. He said he knows people on both sides of the issue and that his position was 'in the middle' (McKenna 2004a: 11).

In May 1999, the British publication *Lancet* – perhaps the most prestigious medical journal in the world – ran a news story reporting the latest dioxin findings from the *Journal of the National Cancer Institute*. It reported on Dr Robert N. Hoover's belief that 'based on the current weight of the evidence … TCDD [the most potent dioxin] should be considered a human carcinogen' (Larkin 1999: 1681). But they found a sceptic in Michigan. Dr Michael Kamrin, a toxicologist from Michigan State University, was quoted as saying that the dioxin data is 'unconvincing and epidemiologically weak. These data don't suggest to me that there's any health risk from dioxin [TCDD]. I didn't think so before, and I don't think so now' (Larkin 1999: 1681). Dr Kamrin later served on Governor Engler's Michigan Environmental Science Board in 1999–2000 where he voted against raising Michigan's standards for protecting children's environmental health.

A Company State?

Does corporate money affect criticism of the benefactors? Michelle Hurd Riddick, with the Lone Tree Council, an environmental group contesting Dow, believes that 'all that Dow money to universities reflects Dow's ability to buy complacency' (McKenna 2004a: 8). There is plenty of money being cast about.

Albion College has been a favourite Dow recipient, owing in part to the fact that Carl Gerstacker, a former CEO of Dow, served on Albion's Board of Directors from 1960 to 1988. Albion received US$3 million in 1997 from the Dow Foundation to upgrade its science facilities. In 2001 the Gerstacker Foundation awarded it another US$2 million to build the Carl A. Gerstacker Liberal Arts Institute for Professional Management. Other small liberal arts colleges have also fared well. In 2002, Hope College received US$1 million to help construct a new science facility. Also in 2002, Alma received US$500,000 for a recreation centre. In 2003 Kalamazoo College received its final instalment of a US$3.2 million gift from the Herbert H. and Grace A. Dow Foundation for its Enlightened Leadership in the 21st Century Initiative. In 1999 Michigan's Hillsdale College received US$500,000 for the Herbert H. Dow II Program in American Journalism. It is 'devoted to the restoration of ethical, high-minded journalism standards and to the reformation of our cultural, political, and social practices' (McKenna 2004a: 11). That year the Dow Program sponsored Richard Lowry, Editor-in-Chief of the *National Review,* as a guest speaker. In his speech, titled 'The High Priests of Journalism: Truth, Morality, and the Media', Lowry criticized American journalism for 'reinforc[ing] the radical side in America's culture wars' (Lowry 2000: 6). He continued:

> What do I mean by the radical side? I am referring to those intellectuals on the Left who are attempting to remold American society and the way we view ourselves as human beings in keeping with an extreme feminist and multicultural world view … [we need to] get more conservatives in journalism, which means supporting projects such as Hillsdale College's "Dow Program in American Journalism" … [and] strengthening institutions that work to change the prevailing culture, from the National Review Institute to conservative institutions in higher education'. (Lowrey 2000: 6)

A full accounting of Dow Chemical's historic involvement in Michigan universities is yet to be written. Such a project would help make transparent a cultural politics that serves corporate interests more than citizen interests. University scholars are well equipped to carry out this research. But will they?

Like Having a Foreign Country in Your Backyard

Dow Chemical is the richest chemical company in United States. With revenues of US$46.3 billion in 2006, Dow Chemical is worth more than 122 of the world's countries according to World Bank statistics. It is like having a foreign country in your own backyard! Would that Dow could be studied like a foreign country, which is what it deserves. Many universities boast area studies programmes that critically investigate the political economy and culture of specific regions of the world, like Africa, Latin America or Asia. It is very common for these programmes to house perspectives that are very critical of capitalism. But, the only sector of the university that regularly studies corporations is business colleges or departments, though they rarely offer a critical perspective. Because Dow is such a big presence at most Michigan universities, its name plastered on buildings and on endowed chairs, it remains off-limits to critical enquiry.

The Importance of Critical Enquiry and Action: True Higher Learning (Is Holistic)

To understand Michigan's dioxin crisis, you must dig into history, gain a fuller appreciation of the stakes involved, study the politics and follow the money. Universities have a name for this: interdisciplinary research. But many academic professionals are reluctant to venture publicly into this issue. When Ryan Bodanyi, Campus Organizer for the International Campaign for Justice in Bhopal, was collecting signatures at the University of Michigan for a 'Resolution in Support of University Disassociation from the Dow Corporation', he was surprised at how few of the faculty signed his petition: 'We approached the Women's Studies department and one person said, "my colleagues might say it's outside our discipline"' (McKenna 2004a: 8). In the public health and health professions fields, there seems to be little excuse not to study the links between the environment and human health. The Herbert H. and Grace A. Dow College of Health Professions at CMU is already committed to 'fostering an understanding of health in its varied dimensions through relevant, community-based experiences' (McKenna 2004a: 13). In the Midland dioxin case, community-based experiences could include rotations with environmentalists from Tittabawassee River Watch, Michigan Department of Environmental Quality fieldworkers, public health nurses, local journalists and citizens living in the polluted areas. Students could also be encouraged to pursue real research projects on Dow and dioxin.

Let us suppose academics from various disciplines got together to pursue research around Dow Chemical's dioxin scandal, as the basis for a book. Communications professionals could diagnose Dow's media manipulation techniques, studying its PR strategies, deceptions and omissions. Political Scientists could look at the 'crisis of democracy', exploring the politics surrounding Dow's influence with governments. Philosophers and political economists might question former Dow CEO Frank Popoff's assertion that 'Growth [is] the opiate we're all hooked on' (Brandt 1997: 575). They could begin by asking simply, 'What is growth?' and unpack it. In fact the philosophers could point out that what Popoff and Brandt call economic 'growth' has a dark side of oppression, pollution and danger. Others might argue a more accurate description is 'capital accumulation' – the real opiate Dow is hooked on.

On the 30th anniversary of a Dow recruiting sit-in at the University of Wisconsin in Madison, two veterans reflected on the event in an article published in Madison's *Capital Times*. Recalling the 5,000 students who were gassed, and 63 who were taken to the hospital, they credited the civil disobedience with 'pushing the anti-war movement beyond the campus and into the community' (Bodden 2006). One of the writers, Paul Soglin, would six years later (1973) be elected mayor of Madison. He served six two-year terms, three in the 1970s and another three in the 1990s (Bodden 2006).

Whereas Brandt argued the Dow sit-ins of the 1960s were mis-directed and a failure because corporate recruitment did not suf-fer, Soglin's reflections were different. The sit-ins galvanized wider opposition to the war and helped to nourish future political lead-ers, like himself. Dissent is a fundamental part of the American project. Just as importantly, active dissent is a fundamental part of identity formation against the forces that would socialize citi-zens to conform and keep quiet. In a 1967 article about the Dow protests, historian Howard Zinn (2003) directed some criticism at the universities. 'The University's acceptance of Dow Chemical re-cruiting as just another business transaction is especially disheart-ening, because it is the University which tells students repeatedly on ceremonial occasions that it hopes students will be more than fact-absorbing automatons, that they will choose humane values, and stand up for them courageously' (Zinn 2003: 307). A new generation has rediscovered this fundamental truth, and again a focus of dissent is Dow Chemical. On 3 December 2003 Dow faced its first nationwide student protests since the Vietnam War. Students from 25 colleges, universities and high schools organized protests around the country against Dow Chemical, as a part of the first-annual Global Day of Action against Corporate Crime. Organisers included Students for Bhopal, Association for India's Development chapters, and the Environmental Justice Program of the Sierra Student Coalition (SSC) (McKenna 2004a: 16). Students delivered contaminated water samples from Bhopal to the homes of 11 of Dow's 14 Board members, including the CEO, William Stavropoulos, and former U-M and Princeton President Harold Shapiro. They asked Dow to accept its moral and legal responsibil-ity for the world's worst industrial disaster. News of these protests was relatively invisible in Michigan media and on Michigan cam-puses (McKenna 2004a: 17).

Summary: Take Back Higher Education

Michigan's Democratic Governor Granholm never seriously chal-lenged Dow Chemical, worried about jobs at a time when the Mich-igan economy ranks near the bottom of the nation. In fact, Dow's power and influence even reaches deeply into the White House. When Mary Gade, a toxicologist and the EPA's top Midwest official (of Region 5, located in Chicago) ordered Dow Chemical in 2008 to begin cleaning up dioxin pollution, the Bush appointee found herself ousted from her job. She was stripped of her powers and told to quit or be fired by 1 June 2008. She resigned. '"There is no question that this is about Dow," Gade said, "I stand behind what I did and what my staff did. I'm proud of what we did"' (Hawthorne 2008). Meanwhile Michigan universities remain relatively quiescent to this powerful leviathan in their backyard. As this article implies, Dow is only one representative of how universities operate as knowledge factories.

Writing is a form of action. As noted, nearly every sentence above was published, in journalistic form, in popular newspaper outlets in Michigan and elsewhere on the Internet. The stories generated much discussion and there were some tangible consequences. I was asked (and accepted) to be the keynote presenter for the three-day 'Backyard ECO Conference 2005' sponsored by Citizens for Alternatives to Chemical Contamination, a group of environmental activists who have been together since 1983. Later they asked me to join their Board of Directors. Also Michelle Hurd-Riddick, a leader of the Lone Tree Council, the central group contesting Dow, informed me that several EPA officials had read my work and had been influenced by it, citing it in their efforts to hold Dow accountable. An April 2009 Google search with the referents 'Dow Chemical' and 'Brian McKenna' generated 609 websites, the great majority of which reproduce these writings. One cannot know what happens to one's writing, but it is comforting to know that some activists in Bhopal were listening. 'I'm really surprised that word about the Dow controversy hasn't reached people in Lansing [until now]', said Satinath Sarangi, with the Bhopal Group for Information and Action (McKenna 2002: 6). The stories are on the www.Bhopal.net webpage.

Social science praxis demands unrelenting public voice about injustice. Required is a radical rupture with a cocooning academic culture and its centripetal rituals. As Eriksen reminded us, anthropologists need to lose their fear of plunging into the controversial issues modern societies present (Eriksen 2006). As muckraking journalism erodes in the face of corporate power, social scientists are among those few professionals with the time, education and power to fill in the cultural gaps by reconstructing their public roles – as border crossers – in addressing the educated lay public. Anthropologists need to become keener participant observers, actors and public writers in their own locales. And they need to begin heuristically studying their own towns and universities as 'company towns'. Our homes are as exotic as anything one might find in the 'Orient'.

References

Aronowitz, S. (2000), *The Knowledge Factory, Dismantling the Corporate University and Creating True Higher Learning* (New York: Beacon Press).

Bledstein, B. J. (1976), *The Culture of Professionalism: The Middle Class and the Development of Higher Education* (New York: Norton).

Bodden, M. (2006), *History of the Mifflin Street Co-op, Madison, WI.* Cited in Paul Soglin's blog: <http://www.waxingamerica.com/2006/05/history_of_the_.Html> (accessed 6 June 2009).

Brandt, E. N. (1997), *Growth Company, DOW Chemical's First Century* (East Lansing: MSU Press).

Doyle, J. (2004), *Trespass Against Us, Dow Chemical and the Toxic Century* (Monroe, ME: Common Courage Press).

Eriksen, T. H. (2006), *Engaging Anthropology, The Case for a Public Presence* (Oxford: Berg).

Giroux, H. (2004), *The Terror of Neoliberalism* (Boulder: Paradigm Publishers).

———— (2007), *University in Chains* (Boulder: Paradigm Publishers).

Hale, C. R. (ed.) (2008), *Engaging Contradictions: Theory, Politics and Methods of Activist Scholarship* (Los Angeles: University of California).

Hawthorne, M. (2008), 'EPA Official Ousted While Fighting Dow', *Chicago Tribune,* 2 May.

Hornblum, A. (1998), *Acres of Skin: Human Experiments at Holmesburg Prison* (New York: Routledge).

Hunt, L. (1991), *Secret Agenda: The United States Government, Nazi Scientists, and Project Paperclip, 1945 to 1990* (New York: St Martins).

IET newsletter (2002), 'IET-affiliated Faculty Will Provide Scientific Expertise to Dow Center for Integrative Technology', *IET Newsletter,* Michigan State University, Spring.

Jacoby, R. (1987), *The Last Intellectuals: American Culture in the Age of Academe* (New York: Noonday).

Kamrin, M. (2003), 'Traces of Environmental Chemicals in the Human Body: Are They a Risk to Health?' *New York: American Council on Science and Health,* 1 May.

Kim, J. Y. (ed.) (2000), *Dying for Growth, Global Inequality and the Health of the Poor* (Monroe: Common Courage Press).

Larkin, M. (1999), 'Public-health Message about Dioxin Remains Unclear', *LANCET* 353 (15 May): 1681.

Lowry, R. (2000), 'The High Priests of Journalism: Truth, Morality, and the Media', *Imprimis* (Hillsdale College), 6.

Martin, T. (2000), 'MSU Weighs Rewards, Risks of Research', *Lansing State Journal,* 17 April: B1, 4.

McKenna, B. (2002), 'Dow, Bhopal and MSU', *Lansing City Pulse,* 27 February, 3, 7.

——— (2003a), 'Education for What? A Chronicle of Environmental Health Deception in Lansing, Michigan', *Cooley Law Review* 20, no. 2: 1–54.

——— (2003b), 'Who is Michigan's Empire Man? Big Ten University President Does Bush's Bidding', *The Free Press* (Ohio), 18 August.

——— (2004a), 'On the Dow Dole, Can Michigan's Universities Be Critical of Chemical Giant'? *From the Ground Up* (Ann Arbor Ecology Center) 1, 7–16 January.

——— (2004b), 'Dow's Knowledge Factories: The MSU Connection', *Lansing City Pulse,* 6 October.

——— (2005), 'Dow Chemical Buys Silence in Michigan, Documentary on Dow's Dioxin Scandal Ignored by Four Local PBS Stations', *CounterPunch,* 18 April.

——— (2008a), 'Conjuring Freire in Dearborn: Higher Ed's "Civic Engagements" Get Dumbed Down', *CounterPunch,* 23 February.

——— (2008b), 'How Dow Chemical Defies Homeland Security and Risks Another 9/11' *CounterPunch,* 20 November.

——— (2008c), 'Ted Downing and Troublemaker Anthropology: How "Yes, Sir," Necessarily Becomes "No sir"', *CounterPunch,* 30 December.

——— (2009), 'How Anthropology Disparages Journalism, Shortchanging Citizens, Damaging Profession', *CounterPunch,* 10 March.

Simcox, R. (2009), *A Degree of Influence: The Funding of Strategically Important Subjects in UK Universities* (London: Center for Social Cohesion).

Swenson, D. (2002), 'Informed Decisions Needed on Dioxin', *Saginaw News,* 9 April.

Washburn, J. (2005), *University, Inc.: The Corporate Corruption of American Higher Education* (New York: Basic).

White, G. (ed.) (2000), *Campus, Inc. Corporate Power in the Ivory Tower* (New York: Prometheus).

Whitehead, D. (1968), *The Dow Story: The History of the Dow Chemical Company* (Texas: McGraw Hill).

Zinn, H. (2003), 'Dow Shall Not Kill', in *The Zinn Reader: Writings on Disobedience and Democracy* (New York: Seven Stories Press), <http://thirdworldtraveler.com/Zinn/Dow_napalm.html> (accessed 6, June 2009).

Producing Knowledge for Public Use
New Challenges in the U.S. Academy

Judith Goode

Recently, I helped to select an honouree for a lifetime achievement of 'actively pursuing the goal of solving human problems using the concepts and tools of social science'[1] awarded by an anthropological organization. Nominee's careers varied and we had to grapple with a vast array of knowledge types, modes of dissemination and ways to measure impact, such as scale (national, global), the numbers of people reached and whether the activity was direct and immediate or indirect and gradual. In 2008, the award was given to Orlando Fals Borda, a Colombian social scientist, for his scholarship on violence in Colombia, his development and sustained global dissemination of a practice called PAR (participatory action research) and his recent co-foundation of a political party shortly before his death. These activities had long marked him as an activist social scientist. This experience brought home to me how our ideas and practices of publicizing anthropology have varied over time, always shaped by particular historic moments. This made me reflect on the differences between the 'public anthropologies' I have experienced from my initiation into the field until today.

As anthropological work has expanded beyond its original focus on the 'non-West' ('the rest') to encompass global processes, there has been an increasing call for a more engaged or 'publicized' anthropology as reflected in this issue as well as, in the case of the U.S., the University of California Press series and several academic Public Anthropology programmes such as those at American University, and the University of Hawaii. What accounts for this intensification of interest now and how does this effort differ from earlier periods of disciplinary efforts to make our knowledge useful?

This article examines changing practices of public anthropology in terms of their new relationship to the political economic processes of global capitalism and neoliberalism as well as changes in the position of anthropology within a hierarchy of knowledge-producing disciplines. Examining my own experiences, first as an anthropologist in the making in the 1960s and then in a faculty role as a North Americanist urban ethnographer training graduate students after the 1970s, I will examine U.S. anthropology's politically variable engagement. I argue that today's call for a public or engaged anthropology partially conflates two seemingly contradictory processes. One is the drive to raise the worth of disciplinary expertise and stake a claim to authority in the world of policy elites in the state, media and academy using their institutional cultures and practices. The other is to communicate theories and methods and through them cogently offer critiques of the very institutions which are gatekeepers for public knowledge in order to reframe public debates.

As our academic work becomes more complex, it focuses not only on the local but on multiple social fields variably embedded within institutional hierarchies. This means that we often find ourselves examining actors in the same professionalized institutional settings in which we ourselves are situated as we seek more authority in them. There are two responses to this paradox. The first is to reformulate our questions and produce knowledge in ways that fit mainstream questions and formats of communication. The second is to invest significant effort in finding ways to help multiple audiences to reframe urgent issues by working on new practices to better convey how power and politics work as complex cultural processes. Should we do both? If so, how can we deal with the contradictions?

The COPP (Committee on Public Policy) of the American Anthropology Association (AAA) was created in the 1990s largely to take on the first purpose, to communicate knowledge to a public policy audience. As an early member and chair of the committee,

I recall discussions and activities focused on understanding what the media wanted and efforts to get policymakers and journalists to call on anthropologists as automatically as they consulted economists and political scientists. The success of this 'branding' of anthropological expertise required us to tailor messages to fit the truncated forms favoured by legislative staff and national advocacy organizations, policy briefs and executive summaries, with numbers and diagrams preferred. Such forms eliminated critical insights about the effects of context, process and contingency. Counting hits on web sites, along with media quotes and sound-bites, become proxies for measuring our impact in spite of our implicit ethnographic sense that we should follow the process through further to explore how information is taken up, reworked and used or rejected.

Reframing critical human issues, those that are globally and nationally urgent in the early twenty-first century, is a more daunting task. Since the 1970s, global and national inequality, instability and violence have grown, become normalized and seen as a 'naturalized' part of the human experience often explained through biological imperatives. Ethnographic work has demonstrated how behavioural and medical expertise overwhelmingly locates blame for critical problems in pathologies of the self or of bad 'cultures', thereby rendering political-economic structuring processes and power relations invisible. Anti-poverty policies that induce instability in the name of economic development work against the social capital that sustains poor families and helps reinforce distrust, the very element that 'civic engagement' theorists argue is the cause of our most pressing problems. Ideas that directly challenge the dominant paradigms of policy experts, popular journalism and mass audiences are not taken up. Some anthropologists like Catherine Besteman and Hugh Gusterson (2005) have tackled reframing public thinking head on through writing pointedly and accessibly for the public, but this is rare.

As we can see from this issue, many other anthropologists engage by directing knowledge to many smaller, more local and intimate audiences. Some model ways to communicate knowledge respectfully to students and 'researched populations' through in-depth, sustained, often face-to-face communication or the use of new electronic and visual media. Recently, several anthropologists have explored communication with their own colleagues in other disciplines with whom they share their professional daily lives (Strathern 2004; Lederman 2006), to explore the boundaries of disciplinary knowledges and ways to cross them.

In the following discussion, I use my early experience with older implicit approaches to the public role of anthropology because these still resonate with the dominant public image and expectations of anthropology and form what our cross-disciplinary colleagues pass on to students in spite of the changed nature of theory, methodology and action. I will then describe the changes I have experienced in my role as an engaged and 'public' urban anthropologist in the last two decades.

Early Academic Training

I was exposed to two very different ideas about the public role of anthropology as an undergraduate at Barnard College/Columbia University in the 1950s where I encountered two conflicting strands of the Boasian legacy. The first was the ethnography of historically particular 'cultures' and the second was Boas' role as a public intellectual confronting the potential uses and misuses of anthropological knowledge to produce progressive change. At Barnard, my mentors emphasized salvage ethnography as natural history to produce academic knowledge of human variation by focusing on the authentic 'ethnographic present'. I especially remember one class in which we read and heard about a timeless way of life in an isolated community all semester, only to be shown slides on the last day showing people with modern clothes, homes, appliances and canned food with no mention of the discrepancy between the two representations of culture.[2]

Recent historical analysis of Boas' 'public' anthropology (Baker 1998, 2008; Pierpont 2004) reveals his role within public debates about concepts of human difference, especially race. Aiming to reframe academic thinking on this critical issue, he was one of the first among his learned colleagues to challenge the hidden

pernicious implications of the scientific racism of his fellow anthropologists. His 'public' was a relatively small academically
educated elite, the academics, professionals and businessmen/phi-
lanthropists who controlled the production and public dissemination of knowledge through exclusive learned societies, museums
and academic institutions like the American Museum of Natural
History.

Across the street from Barnard, in the Columbia General Studies
programme, undergraduates flocked to one of Boas' well-known
students, Margaret Mead, who along with Ruth Benedict had carried on the drive to provide useful information for the nation or to
educate the public about particular family anxieties. For example,
both Mead and Benedict had earlier participated in the dissemination of anthropology directed toward the U.S. war and post-war
effort: Benedict through *The Chrysanthemum and the Sword* (1946),
a profile of Japanese 'national character', and Mead through an
episode of working as the leader of the National Research Council
food habits research for use in preparing to feed city populations
who might be evacuated. In my college years, Mead (and Benedict)
had expanded their publics by cultivating the post-war growth of
U.S. college-educated professionals as a mass audience for their
best-selling ethnographies and their regular columns related to
childrearing and attitudes about sexuality in *Redbook,* a popular
magazine for women. Later, Mead became a leader in exploring
the use of documentary film as a form of communicating with
the public. Their expansion of a popular audience had indirectly
influenced many of us to enter the field.

Looking back to this time and place reveals an anthropology
which un-self-consciously engaged in producing knowledge for
its own sake, as well as making it useful for the educated elite by
providing a comparative view of human nature which was shaped
to address middle-class anxieties or to serve the nation in wartime.
Obligations to publicize and make their findings useful for those
whom they studied who were viewed as located 'outside' time
and the West were missing, as revealed by the subsequent PBS
Nova series *Anthropology on Trial* which was part of the post-1960s
critical turn.

The Modernization/Development Paradigm

Moving on to Cornell University for doctoral studies, the world shifted. Here I encountered emphasis on the active, direct use of knowledge to produce change directly emerging within a new post-war technocratic optimism for 'policy science', which advocated using expert knowledge to engineer solutions to social problems. Policy science took on a mantle of 'objectivity' and 'value neutrality' through the use of probabilistic models and quasi-experimental research designs. In anthropology, this shift, as well as earlier wartime efforts, led to the self-conscious institutionalization of applied anthropology in the 1940s.

At Cornell, applied anthropology converged with the as yet unacknowledged relationship between the university and the Cold War state (O'Mara 2005). The state, as well as private foundations, supported the training of area studies experts through the National Defense Education Act or Ford Foundation programmes in area studies which supported 'soft' social science research both to 'modernize' and 'develop' the 'third world' in order to prevent insurgency, or, in the case of some work funded by the U.S. Department of Defense, to look explicitly for social indicators to predict insurgency (Wolf and Jorgenson 1970; Horowitz 1970). These projects paralleled the more visible 'hard' science research for Cold War defence.

In that moment, before the wide spread of post-1960s critical awareness which spotlighted critical theories of power, class, race and gender as well as theories of world systems and dependency, the Cornell-Peru Project, in Vicos Peru, directed by Alan Holmberg (Isbell this issue) used the literature of policy science to justify 'participant intervention' (Holmberg 1955) or linked research *and* 'development' in one methodology (Holmberg 1958). Replacing cultural relativity with eight 'universal' values or rights derived from Harold Lasswell, a pioneer in policy science, Holmberg and other applied anthropologists who were trying to stake a claim to membership in policy science, clearly accepted the scientific requirements of neutrality, objectivity and experimentalism by accepting its terms while attempting to justify and minimize the difficulties in reconciling ethnography and science.

This approach was markedly different from my undergraduate experiences in which both the impact of political economic transformation on the 'researched' as well as their capacity as consumers of knowledge was ignored in the name of cultural relativity. On the other hand, the project's paternalistic top-down approach emphasized 'techniques' for managing change through which those outside history and modernity needed to be culturally manipulated to be moved minimally 'inside' before knowledge could be shared or co-produced in a participatory, collaborative way. In this case, the non-reflexive use of ethnographic knowledge to facilitate the entry and positioning of the project leaders at the top of the hacienda power hierarchy clearly dates the project as coming before the discipline's widespread concern with power relations, and political critique.

Furthermore, by ignoring the impact of outside political economic structures in which the Vicos hacienda was embedded, the project constructed the community as isolated and living in a functionalist equilibrium. This was depicted in the widely shown film, *So That Men Are Free,* (Van Dyke 1962) made by CBS films which publicized the project and emphasized the triumphal heroic success of anthropology in bringing a group of peasants, described as living the same life they have since the sixteenth-century Spanish conquest, into the modern world. The effects of inattention to theories and actualities of power relations, regional, national and global politics or world systems was brought home when neighbouring hacienda residents, influenced by Vicosinos, began political action against their masters. They were met with violent reprisals by the hacienda owners and the state.

While varying in approach as to how anthropological knowledge should be deployed to bring about change, both of my formative academic settings were steeped in an earlier pre-critical anthropology that did not question or foreground issues of power and politics in knowledge production. Without a self-conscious critique of the ethics and politics of research and representation or a reflexive conceptualization of how to use knowledge for various publics, we did not anticipate the unintended outcomes of anthropology put to use.

Attending to Power: Critical Anthropology

The experience of 'publicizing', or making knowledge useful to the public, was very different in the first two decades of my work in the academy, roughly 1970 to 1990. It differed both from what had come before 1970 and from my experiences after 1990. In the following two sections, I will discuss these changes and their implications for the possibility of developing audiences or publics located in different positions in the local milieu in which I work.

The effects of several simultaneous and linked global engagements begun earlier: the Cold War, postcolonial movements, and domestic movements focused on race and gender inequality in the U.S., along with the importation of critical theories of power new to U.S. cultural anthropology, transformed views of research populations in the 1970s. Former bearers of self-contained 'cultures' became subjects of 'third-world' nations. The circulation of Marxist, feminist, anti-racist and postcolonial and post-structural critiques within anthropology and other disciplines signalled a sea change in the field as I began urban research on Philadelphia in the 1970s, soon joined by colleagues and students whose places of training had been infused with the 'new wave'. While evocations of timeless 'traditional culture' still marked discourses of development practice (Edelman and Haugerud 2005, the justifications for incorporating new scales of urban, national and global political economies into our work grew. The practice of contextualizing ethnographic work within scales of structural power moved front and centre in ethnographic practice. The implications for the politics and ethics of research were subjected to heated debates at contentious American Anthropological Association (AAA) meetings, and in critical volumes like *Reinventing Anthropology* (Hymes 1972) throughout the 1970s. Debates centred on the power relations and responsibilities of ethnographers to the people they studied, as well as forcing a recognition of the unacknowledged implications of research in 'hot spots' whether they were framed as 'pure' and generated by theory or overtly complicit in counterinsurgency research (Wolf and Jorgensen 1970; Horowitz 1970).

Moreover, as Laura Nader (1972) exhorted us to 'study up', and urban anthropologists like Anthony Leeds (1994) exhorted ethnographers to place populations within nested power hierarchies and to look at dynamic intersections of structure, culture and agency, these issues became central to the critiques of the 'culture of poverty' as well as the early critiques of the use of 'traditional' culture to explain the failure of development projects.

These debates moved ethnography towards incorporating both theories of power relations as well as ethnographies of encounters between ordinary people and institutions of power (e.g. Susser 1982). Anthropological discourse, before multi-scaled and multi-sited ethnography was seriously addressed, usually deployed a simplified dichotomy between two monoliths: the relatively unexamined 'powerful' and the 'powerless' – our normative research subjects.

Moreover, with the publication of many strong critiques of the 'culture of poverty' (Stack 1974; Leacock 1971; Eames and Goode 1977), many of us, not yet familiar with theories of power and knowledge relationships, were still steeped in a liberal belief that simply producing research and making it available would magically change hearts and minds. Scholars like Stack learned first hand about the political and epistemological barriers which existed as she struggled to publicize her findings, which directly challenged politically privileged presuppositions.

Philadelphia Public Anthropology: 1970 to 1990

As a faculty member at Temple University since the 1970s, my research agenda along with many Temple doctoral students has focused on the structural production of poverty and inequality in the city of Philadelphia and on the political use of raced, nativist and class-marked discourses to (mis)represent and divide the downwardly mobile residents stranded by late capitalism. As critics of the persistence of the 'culture of poverty' concept, our work encompassed poor people's politics: resistance and social movements (Goode and Maskovsky 2001).

As the discipline continuously reframed its theoretical and methodological engagement with broader-scaled political economic structuring processes and the nexus of power and knowledge, our work became more complex as we added new institutional sites, multi-sited designs, and situated the work within emerging paradigms such as urban anthropology, North American anthropology, the anthropology of policy and transnational/global studies.

When our research populations were limited to the 'powerless' and our frameworks were less complex, efforts at publicizing knowledge were easier since there was less disagreement over the 'common sense' constructions of the problems of deindustrialization between anthropologists and those with whom we worked: colleagues in the academy, university administrations as well as city government and social service agencies.

Philadelphia's reform project in the 1960s and 1970s was conceived very differently from today. What we now recognize as state-sponsored gentrification, and privatised uneven development (Smith 1996), redevelopment was discussed through national, not global Keynesian/Fordist frameworks. Deindustrialization was reversible if addressed through increasing the tax base and public investment. We counted on local political mobilizations to influence the priorities for such technocratic 'fixes' to generate jobs, and regenerate public services (Goode, 2010).

At Temple University, researchers worked in interdisciplinary collaborations engaged in common cause. Two sets of research groups of faculty members in social sciences and humanities focused on the material, social and ethical effects of plant-closings and produced conferences, media coverage and two books (Raines et al. 1982; Hochner et al. 1988).

Temple at this time was a hospitable setting for this research. This urban university, located in the centre of an increasingly black and poor North Philadelphia, had an original populist mission of social uplift. It had served, inadvertently, as a key space for social movement organizing related to the civil rights and welfare rights movements (Countryman 2006). The administration had stood up to a threatened withdrawal of its new state funding stream, in the early days of its new status as one of three 'state-related' universities in Pennsylvania, when it insisted on hosting the national convention of the Black Panther Party in 1970 after the group was denied access to all the traditional convention venues in the city (Wachman 2005). In the 1970s, in response to a community protest against university expansion and low-income housing loss, the university had organized formal negotiations which resulted in halting new demolition and providing concessions related to access to public space, recreational facilities and the creation of a popular education institute.

Moreover, community organizing and social mobilizations were common within all the researched 'communities' with whom we worked as they engaged in linked citywide networks of neighbourhood action against downtown development, highway projects and encroaching gentrification (Goode and Schneider 1994; Goode and O'Brien 2006). In the spirit of responsibility to researched populations, anthropology and urban studies students worked alongside community organizers and neighbourhood umbrella organizations, to provide data and research skills to CBOs (community based organizations), to help them stay in front of real-estate housing speculation through mapping, acquiring and rehabilitating abandoned housing and to help create land trusts, write grants for competitive federally funded Community Development Block Grant programmes and to lobby for laws such as the Community Reinvestment Act to prevent banks from refusing to make home loans in poor neighbourhoods.

Within the Philadelphia Changing Relations Project in the late 1980s (Goode and Schneider 1994; Bach 1993; Goode 1998), teams of graduate and undergraduate students looked at the role of local organizations and city agencies in ameliorating or exacerbating tension between new immigrants and established poor white or racialised populations. The project provided insights about the unintended effects of multicultural programming (Goode 2005) and we publicized our findings widely to community residents, leaders of CBOs, front-line social service providers, city agencies and community leaders and residents through conferences, local and city media, lectures, op-ed pieces, and court testimony (Goode and Schneider 1994).

These two decades produced many instances of dissemination through one-time mass media forays into 'public anthropology' as well as many sustained collaborations with communities resulting in recommendations to prevent unintended consequences and misunderstandings between communities and service providers.

Globalism, Neoliberalism and Higher Stakes: 1990s to Present

In the last two decades, global inequalities, instability, violence and the U.S. public's sense of urgency have grown to new levels as contradictions between culturally constructed ideals of peace, equality, social justice, and democracy, increasingly diverge from social practice in frightening ways (Lutz 2001; Gill 2000; Maskovsky 2001; Collins et al. 2008) leading to calls for the primacy of ethical (Scheper Hughes 1990) and activist anthropology (Lyon-Callo 2004).

Simultaneously the theoretical models and methods of anthropology have broadened in scale to incorporate local, national, transnational and global scales simultaneously. By the 1990s, such concepts as globalization, transnationalism and neoliberalism had been theorized and ethnographically demonstrated sufficiently to complicate the simple black-and-white dichotomy between the powerful and powerless. The simple dichotomy was replaced with a desire to demonstrate ethnographically how power works through relationships between and within contested institutions and everyday life and to document the processes through which individual political subjectivity shapes and is shaped by discourse.

These paradigm shifts were linked to what was happening 'on the ground', in other words the material and discursive shifts shaping and being shaped by the rollback of the Keynesian/Fordist regime and the rollout of neoliberal and global discourse and practice (Harvey 2005). The critiques of neoliberalism foregrounded the displacement of Keynesian justifications of public investment and social welfare (by neoliberal privatisation), the withdrawal of state provisioning, and market solutions alongside discourses of personal responsibility, and the triumphal celebration of individuals who had successfully adopted neoliberal personas by making 'good' choices alongside escalating the blame and punishment for those who made 'bad' choices (Kingfisher 2002). There were many politically demobilizing effects produced by the new public/private relationships as well (Goode and Maskovsky 2001), leading to calls for an 'activist' engaged anthropology.

At the same time, anthropologists joined others (e.g. O'Connor 2001) in finding new ways to look at the politics of knowledge production and the effects of intentional technocratic 'policy science' and 'social engineering' on sociopolitical relations. The critical work of James Ferguson (1994) on development policy in Lesotho demonstrated that what was really important was not the explanation of why development fails but the ethnographic analysis of the productive nature of policy in practice. Looking at what programmes actually created as 'side effects' or instrument effects was a key to understanding how power and politics generated action and structure in situations of change. What happened could not be understood within the framework of the techno-scientific apparatus of 'development' but had everything to do with existing political relations and political practice that is made invisible in the neutral professional discourse and practice of policy. Shore and Wright (1998) called for an anthropology of policy that uncovered the diagnosis problems in the off-the-mark blame discourses inherent in cultural constructions of policy targets, while Fisher (1997) through a review of ethnographic evidence about the workings of NGO advocacy groups raised questions about whether they were uniformly 'doing good' and about the variable links between NGOs and power structures.

As Temple students and colleagues mutually began to work within these frameworks which incorporated ways of addressing the operation of power through discourse, governmentality, 'expertise' and the coercive effects of 'audit culture' (Strathern 2000), our focus shifted from the 'grass roots' to social locations in the junctures where power-laden, multi-scalar institutions encounter city residents. Ethnographies like those of Gregory (1998) and Checker (2005) model linkages between historical process and encounters between differently located agents deploying varying discourses and political subjectivities.

New research developed by anthropology faculty members, postdoctoral and pre-doctoral students began to examine how neoliberalism, working through multiple local public/private economic development programmes and educational privatisation projects, sponsored by state, market and civil society institutions, affected the civic engagement and politics of the poor (e.g. Hyatt 2001; Hyatt and Peebles 2003; Goode 2005, 2006; Maskovsky 2000, 2001, 2006; Goode and O'Brien 2006; Hardy 2006; Roaf 2007; Suess 2008).

These new frameworks were productive sources of new insights, but had the paradoxical effect of implicating and alienating our closest colleagues who, in spite of presumed similarity in social location, were following different intellectual pathways. Critical findings were more likely to be ignored, misunderstood or actively rejected not because of the old complaints about anthropology's complicity with power elites but because we raised questions about more privileged sectors. Our colleagues would see themselves as implicated in the unintended effects of policy and this challenged the value of their expertise and their sense of themselves as well-intentioned problem solvers. That these actors and organizations were also experiencing loss of respect and caught in increasingly bureaucratized structures of constraint and accountability did not help. New paradigms created 'noise' and communicative distance between us and the more literal straightforward analysis of those with whom we had collaborated in city agencies, the academy, the media and local organizations. It was easier to reject the new frameworks as mystifying and anthropologists as arrogant and self-aggrandizing.

I observed the same actors who I have collaborated with for decades shifting their alliances as their organizations, whether local community, city government or academically based, restructured and took on neoliberal governance practices. Some local organizations were incorporated into new public/private power structures while others tried to mobilize political opposition. In the process, strong friendships and alliances were destroyed (Goode and O'Brien 2006). Similar political fault lines and epistemological disconnections grew in the university between faculty and administrators around the discursive and coercive effects of expertise and bureaucracy. Disagreements occurred within departments, and between Liberal Arts disciplines and professional or practitioner fields. At the same time, work speed-up left few opportunities to deal in-depth with these conflicts.

Unlike Boas who was offering a critique based on specialized knowledge and data acknowledged as 'anthropological' to demonstrate a distinction between race, culture and language or Holmberg who was contributing the normalized ethnographic knowledge of the 'indigenous' to a 'science of policy' as well as the interdisciplinary projects in neighbourhoods combining expected anthropological knowledge about 'exotics at home' with other disciplinary knowledge, new paradigms went against the grain for many publics. Expert colleagues, whose basic epistemologies were being challenged, along with the public-at-large could openly disagree with what seemed to be over-analysed and often mistaken interpretations of their own interpreted experience. Contemplating possibilities for bridging the gap in cultural constructions between long-term colleagues in academic and community circles was discomforting.

Distance widened even more as the city and university were caught up in rescaling projects to become 'global'. Neoliberal practices were widely deployed by the city and university throughout the 1990s as the public school system was 'privatised' and new forms of management and governmentality emphasized technologies of self-management, created exaggerated ritual celebrations of success and turned knowledge into technical skills (Urciuoli 2006) while at the same time consolidating the level of the bureaucratic and ritual apparatus of 'audit' culture (Strathern 2000). These trends sacralise the truth-value and precision of metrics and mapping, and fail to distinguish between actualities that are better captured through contingent, contextualized and qualitative forms of analysis. In terms of those with clout in the 'information economy' there was a cost-benefit deficit as well as a political disadvantage linked to complex critical analysis.

This was especially true at a public urban university like Temple in which the rapidly growing number and size of vocational and professional schools and faculties now dominate (Goode 2008). Subject to centralized accrediting agencies and marketing credentials of expertise, certainty trumps critique, now seen at best, as a nostalgic emblem of the Golden Age of the professoriate and at worst as the target of the movement against academic freedom.

As state funding shrank, Temple became more enrolment driven and pushed to upscale its student body and its physical plant. It also became enmeshed in property development as part of the city's campaign to rescale itself as a 'global' city. The city and university worked in tandem to attract capital investment to the city and neighbourhood (ibid.). This once again changed the relationship between the university and its surrounding residential communities.

In this effort, university collaborations with the city and surrounding neighbourhoods were expanded and consolidated for new capital investment. 'Civilizing missions' through mechanisms like: 'partnerships' engaged in collaborations to beautify and landscape the environment, a School District contract to operate local schools, and the creation of medical and social extension services via clinics that also trained professional students. Most of all, a variety of incentives were given to develop community-based learning through recruiting student volunteers as interns and service learners. Some of these efforts were intellectual efforts at critical pedagogy such as the class which produced *The Death and Rebirth of North Philadelphia* (Hyatt and Peebles 2003) or the *In and Out* programme created by Lori Pompa. Others were part of the university's neoliberal project of development. Often both interests wrestled for dominance in these endeavours.

The 'ears to the ground' ethnographic perspective on what was happening increasingly diverged from those of former colleagues and friends who had major stakes in programmes that became co-opted by the university. They often experienced the same everyday happenings, but interpreted them differently through lenses shaped by their professional training and position. Our views were silenced more by a lack of time or discursive space in which to examine mutually the diverging assumptions and frameworks about these projects. While anthropologists have recently begun to explore new ways to discuss difference with those in other knowledge-producing disciplines, the elite university contexts they describe are protected by specific institutional resource investments (Strathern 2004) or by the privileged elite working conditions of universities whose 'brand' is premised on space for 'Ivory Tower' contemplation (Lederman 2006). The working conditions and frequent resource emergencies in publicly funded urban universities in the U.S. often work against this. Such increasing obstacles to reaching across disciplinary boundaries leads many anthropologists to turn inward and to talk, publish and read in smaller networks amongst those who share their paradigms.

Conclusion

Before the Second World War, U.S. anthropology's public was an elite audience seeking authoritative knowledge, within which Boas, as an outsider, struggled to become authoritative. His students were authorities to the state and nation at war and then spoke to a new mass middle-class audience through mass media. Some anthropologists who sought to enter a new technocratic policy elite in 'development' and 'modernization' and with varying degrees of self-awareness, were drawn into Cold War research.

Following the critical reaction of the 1970s, engendered by the as yet under-theorized forces of 'globalization' and 'neoliberalism', analysis shifted to political economic, post-colonial, feminist and post-structural critiques, placing power at the centre of analysis. This disciplinary crisis pushed anthropologists to address power issues reflexively, to work more closely with research populations as the first audience for their understandings, and to question their role vis-à-vis dominant political and economic structures. Moreover, the last decades of the twentieth century saw anthropologists working on problems in networks and institutions socially located outside the nation state, and framed their work and its dissemination in terms of multiple levels of scale and multiple socio-spatial sites.

Meanwhile, in the U.S. academy the very global neoliberal conditions which produced the critique also fortified the pre-existing strong preference for certainty, predictability and simplicity (e.g. rational choice models) of the positivist and metrically oriented segments of social sciences consumed by political and corporate elites. Ethnography provided evidence that demonstrated how and why politically inflected cultural constructions shape the explanations of 'social problems' held by institutional actors and individual citizens, and the corresponding policy fixes they imply. These presuppositions undermine important insights about power and politics ultimately undermining attempts to challenge portrayals of inequality, instability and militarisation as 'natural', 'normal' human conditions to be valued as 'opportunities' for reinvention and spiritual ennoblement. Just as the unintended political effects of this kind of knowledge production as well as the ways it could be appropriated by specific political projects has been increasingly laid bare and challenged by interpretative historic and ethnographic analysis, the value of theorised anthropological analysis has been diminished especially in universities with vocational market-oriented missions.

I now turn back to the paradoxical issue of whether and how we can and should continue to 'publicize' anthropology's analytic usefulness through simplified formats and techniques that overlook context and contingency in order to raise our standing as experts without undermining the attempt to create new insights and processual ways of thinking about problems in an increasingly perilous world. The latter understandings require denser, less portable formats and an emphasis on contingency and process. This requires more effort at tracing the ethical contradictions and instrumental effects of speaking to the media about particular issues while at the same time searching for the rare social settings in which we can do the reframing work with variable potential audiences.

There are several reasons for doing both kinds of work. First, it is important to brand public anthropology and raise the profile and the authority of the discipline in a world in which information comes in 'bits' and attention spans have been shaped by sound bites and a preference for de-contextualized magic numbers. This can work while we still maintain a critical edge and avoid the 'evil twin' evoked by Ferguson (2005).[3] In the U.S., academic public anthropology efforts teach us about communicating to the policy and media worlds through their preferred formats and protocols for communicating. At the same time, the national AAA campaign to publicize anthropological insights on race is using current knowledge for a blockbuster public exhibit placed in valued cultural spaces thereby paralleling Boas' public anthropology. This works to provide the museum-going public with critical information to challenge racism. This informs as well as legitimises the authority of the discipline on a crucial public issue while also demonstrating that we no longer specialize in representing the exotic other (Di Leonardo 1998).

Yet, at the same time, we must also be impelled to reframe other public political debates, and political action in terms of politically and structurally inflected paradigms. The simultaneous attempt to cater to existing media channels while we pay attention to encouraging complex perspectives from many social locations will directly expose pernicious ethical and conceptual contradictions between the two, and help identify and transcend specific epistemological, structural and political obstacles to audience acceptance. Complex reframing calls for smaller, more intimate social spaces with differential strategies to focus on specific kinds of epistemological obstacles: simplistic master narratives, scientific certainty, correlations interpreted as understandings of cause and effect and other forms of 'truth' which extend the reach of neoliberal 'common sense'.

This is the place which calls for recommendations of strategies and examples of successes in communicating across the intellectual boundaries we confront. Yet as specialists who privilege a focus on contingencies and context, our work makes processual case specificities the heart of the matter, precluding simple prescriptions. Some life-threatening health and environmental issues can be addressed by public programmes, such as Maida's contributions to public health, where changing behaviour can have spectacular results without structural change (Maida, Part 1 this issue). But our witnessing, documenting and analysing the fall out of contemporary human-made structural processes yields a sense of urgency. We must continue to render transparent the invisible political processes which underlie the production of contemporary inequality. The trick is to use our common social practice of identifying potential allies in various sites along the broad spectrum of socio-spatial and network scales and take the time necessary to communicate complexity. Especially important publics today are our closest neighbours in the academy itself.

Acknowledgements

I would like to thank all my mentors who taught me to be committed to the people with whom we engage anthropologically and inspired me to broaden my horizons, especially Catherine McClellan and Alan Holmberg. Since intellectual productivity is profoundly social, my peer community at Temple anthropology has been crucial to my rethinking. Tom Patterson and many wonderful students, especially Jeff Maskovsky, inspired me to engage with new literatures. Most recently, my generous young colleagues, Susan Hyatt, Sydney White and Jessica Winegar have introduced me to new ideas. Similarly, the communities of two sections of the AAA: SANA (Society for the Anthropology of North America) and SUNTA (Society for Urban, National and Transnational Anthropology) have been crucial as well. Support for the research discussed in this article came from the Ford Foundation 'Changing Relations Project' (1988–1990) and the Cultural Anthropology Program of the National Science Foundation for 'Poverty and Civic Participation in Three Urban Communities in Philadelphia' (1999–2001).

Notes

1. The Bronislaw Malinowski award of the Society for Applied Anthropology
2. Ironically, several of my friends and I had been late converts to anthropology because it promised a more comprehensive 'history' of human life, but found ourselves studying 'timelessness'.
3. Ferguson argues there is a fundamental and irreconcilable contradiction between knowledge produced by those who critique the assumptions of development institutions and that produced by those who work within them

References

Bach, R. (1993), *Changing Relations: Newcomers and Established Residents in U.S. Communities* (New York: Ford Foundation).

Baker, L. (1998), *From Savage to Negro: Anthropology and the Construction of Race 1896 to 1954* (Berkeley: University of California Press).

——— (2008), 'History of Anthropology', in *Encyclopedia of Race and Racism*, (ed.) J. H. Moore (New York: Macmillan Reference).

Benedict, R. (1946), *The Chrysthanthemum and the Sword: Patterns of Japanese Culture* (Boston: Houghton Mifflin).

Besteman, C. and Gusterson, H. (2005), *Why America's Top Pundits are Wrong: Anthropologists Talk Back* (Berkeley: University of California Press).

Checker, M. (2005), *Polluted Promises: Environmental Racism and the Search for Social Justice in a Southern Town* (New York: NYU Press).

Collins, J., Di Leonardo, M. and Williams, B. (eds.) (2008), *New Landscapes of Inequality* (Santa Fe: SAR Press).

Countryman, M. (2006), *Up South: Civil Rights and Black Power in Philadelphia* (Philadelphia: University of Pennsylvania Press).

Di Leonardo, M. (1998), *Exotics at Home: Anthropologies, Others and American Modernity* (Chicago: University of Chicago Press).

Eames, E. and J. Goode (1977) *The Anthropology of the City: An Introduction to Urban Anthropology* (Englewood Cliffs, NJ: Prentice Hall)

Edelman, M. and A. Haugerud (eds.) (2005), *The Anthropology of Development and Globalization: From Classical Economy to Contemporary Neoliberalism* (Oxford: Blackwell).

Ferguson, J. (1994), *The Anti-politics Machine: 'Development', Depoliticization, and Bureaucratic Power in Lesotho* (Minneapolis: University of Minnesota Press).

—— (2005), 'Anthropology and Its Evil Twin: 'Development' in the Constitution of a Discipline', in *The Anthropology of Development and Globalization*, (eds.) M. Edelman and A. Haugerud (Oxford, Blackwell Publishing).

Fisher, W. (1997), 'Doing Good? The Politics and Anti-politics of NGO Practices', *Annual Review of Anthropology* 26: 439–464.

Gill, L. (2000), *Teetering on the Rim: Global Restructuring, Daily Life and the Armed Retreat of the Bolivian State* (New York: Columbia University).

Goode, J. (1998), 'The Contingent Construction of Local Identities: Koreans and Puerto Ricans in Philadelphia', *Identities* 5, no. 1: 33–64.

—— (2005), 'Dousing the Fire or Fanning the Flames: The Role of Human Relations Practice in Inter-group Conflict', *Transforming Anthropology* 13, no. 1: 41–53.

—— (2006), 'Faith-based Organizations in Philadelphia: Neoliberal Ideology and the Decline of Political Activism', *Urban Anthropology* 35: 203–236.

—— (2008), 'Reinventing Temple: The Second Time's the Charm', Paper presented at the Festschrift honoring Thomas C. Patterson, Tenth Annual Meeting of the Society for the Anthropology of North America.

—— (2010), 'The Campaign for New Immigrants in Philadelphia: Imagining Possibilities and Confronting Realities', in *Locating Migra-*

tion: The Migrant and Urban Scale, (eds.) N. Glick Schiller and A. Calgar (Ithaca, New York: Cornell University Press).

Goode, J. and Maskovsky, J. (eds.) (2001), *New Poverty Studies: The Ethnography of Politics, Policy, and Immiseration in the United States* (New York: NYU Press).

Goode, J. and O'Brien, R. T. (2006), 'Whose Social Capital? How Economic Development Projects Disrupt Local Social Relations', in *Social Capital in Philadelphia,* (ed.) R. Dilworth, III (Philadelphia: Temple University Press), 159–176.

Goode, J. and Schneider, J. A. (1994), *Reshaping Ethnic and Racial Relations in Philadelphia: Immigrants in a Divided City* (Philadelphia: Temple University Press).

Gregory, S. (1998), *Black Corona: Race and the Politics of Place in a Black Community* (Princeton: Princeton University Press).

Hardy, L. J. (2006), 'Pets and the Expression of Class, Race and Gender Tensions in an Upscaling Neighbourhood' (PhD diss., Temple University).

Harvey, D. (2005), *A Brief History of Neoliberalism* (New York: Oxford University Press).

Hochner, A., Goode, J., Granrose, C., Simon, E. and Appelbaum, E. (1988), *Job-saving Strategies: Worker Buyouts and Quality Work Life* (Kalamazoo, MI: The W.E. Upjohn Institute for Employment Research).

Holmberg, A. (1955), 'Participant Intervention in the Field', *Human Organization* 14, no. 11: 23–26.

——— (1958), 'The Research and Development Approach to the Study of Change', *Human Organization* 17, no. 3: 12–16.

Horowitz, I. L. (1970), 'The Life and Death of Project Camelot', *Transaction* 3, no. 1: 2–10.

Hyatt, S. B. (2001), 'From Citizen to Volunteer: Neoliberal Governance and the Erasure of Poverty', in *New Poverty Studies: The Ethnography of Politics, Policy, and Immiseration In The United States,* (eds.) J. Goode and J. Maskovsky (New York: NYU Press).

Hyatt, S. B. and Peebles, P. (eds.) (2003), 'The Death and Rebirth of North Central Philadelphia' (Philadelphia: Renaissance Community Development Corporation).

Hymes, D. (1972), *Reinventing Anthropology* (New York: Pantheon).

Kingfisher, C. (2002) *Western Welfare in Decline: The Feminization of Poverty,* (Philadelphia: University of Pennsylvania Press).

Leacock, E. B. (ed.) (1971), *The Culture of Poverty: A Critique.* New York: Touchstone.

Lederman, R. (2006), 'The Perils of Working at Home: IRB "Mission creep" as Context and Content for an Ethnography of Disciplinary Knowledge', *American Ethnologist* 33: 482–491.

Leeds, A. (posthumously edited by Roger Sanjek) (1994), *Cities, Classes and the Social Order* (Ithaca, NY: Cornell University Press).

Lutz, C. (2001), *Homefront: A Military City and the American Twentieth Century* (Boston: Beacon Press).

Lyon-Callo, V. (2004), *Inequality, Poverty, and Neoliberal Governance: Activist Ethnography in the Homeless Sheltering Industry* (Ontario: Broadview Press).

Maskovsky, J. (2000), '"Managing" the Poor: Neoliberalism, Medicaid HMOs and the Triumph of Consumerism Among the Poor', *Medical Anthropology* 19: 121–146.

—— (2001), 'The Other War at Home', *Urban Anthropology* 30: [215-238].

—— (2006), 'Governing the New Hometowns: Race, Power and Neighborhood Participation in the New Inner City', *Identities* 13, 73–99.

Nader, L. (1972) 'Up the Anthropologist: Perspectives Gained from Studying Up' in *Reinventing Anthropology* (ed.) D. Hymes (New York: Pantheon Books), 284–311.

O'Connor, A. (2001), *Social Science, Social Policy and the Poor in Twentieth Century U.S. History* (Princeton: Princeton University Press).

O'Mara, M. P. (2005), *Cities of Knowledge: Cold War Science and the Search for the Next Silicon Valley* (Princeton: Princeton University Press).

PBS video (1970), 'Anthropology on Trial' NOVA series, Margaret Mead episode.

Pierpont, C. R. (2004), 'The Measure of America', *The New Yorker* (20 August).

Raines, J., Berson, L. and Gracie, D. (eds.) (1982), *Capital and Community in Conflict: Plant Closings and Job Loss* (Philadelphia: Temple Univeristy Press).

Roaf, M. (2007), *Choice for All?: Contradictions in Charter School Policies and Practices,* (PhD diss., Temple University).

Scheper Hughes, N. (1990), 'The Primacy of the Ethical: Propositions for a Militant Anthropology', *Current Anthropology* 36, 409–440.

Shore, C. and S. Wright (eds.) (1997) *Anthropology of Policy,* (New York: Routledge).

Smith, N. (1996), *The New Urban Frontier: Gentrification and the Revanchist City* (London: Routledge).

Stack, C. (1974) *All Our Kin: Strategy for Survival in a Black Community,* (New York: Harper and Row).

Strathern, M. (ed.), (2000), *Audit Cultures: Anthropological Studies in Accountability, Ethics and the Academy* (London: Routledge).

––––––– (2004), *Commons and Borderlands: Working Papers on Interdisciplinarity Accountability and the Flow of Knowledge* (Oxford: Sean Kingston Publishing).

Suess, G. E. L. (2008), 'Beyond School Walls: The Politics of Community and Place in Two Philadelphia Neighborhoods' (PhD diss., Temple University).

Susser, I. (1982), *Norman Street: Poverty and Politics in an Urban Neighborhood* (New York: Oxford University Press).

Urciuoli, B. (2006), 'Strategically Deployable Shifters in College Marketing, or Just What Do They Mean by "Skills", "Leadership" and "Multiculturalism"?' *Language and Culture: Symposium 6.*

Van Dyke, W. (1962) (dir.) *So that Men are Free,* (New York: CBS News/ McGraw Hill Films). Accessible 9.11.2009 from: http://courses.cit .cornell.edu/vicosperu/vicos-site/cornellperu_page_1.htm

Wachman, M. (2005), *The Education of a University President* (Philadelphia: Temple University Press).

Wolf, E. and Jorgensen, J. (1970), 'Anthropology on the Warpath in Thailand', *New York Review of Books* 9 (November): 26–35.

Notes on a Dialogical Anthropology

Udi Mandel Butler

Publics in Anthropology

Since the birth of the discipline many anthropologists have been concerned with the potential practical uses of their knowledge. Indeed the term 'applied anthropology' has been attributed to the British anthropologist Pitt-Rivers who used it as far back as 1881 (Gardner and Lewis 1996). But right from the beginning the issue of *who* should benefit from such knowledge has been a controversial one. For some, like Boas and his students, the new discipline of anthropology was to provide a scientific basis to ward off evolutionist racist theories (see Eriksen 2006). At the same time, over the first half of the twentieth century, a number of anthropologists worked alongside colonial administrators and their knowledge was used, to varying degrees, to further colonial rule (Asad 1973). In the postcolonial period controversies surrounding anthropological knowledge in the U.S. have been associated with U.S. government counter-insurgency, the most notorious being Project Camelot (Wolf and Jorgensen 1970). Such controversial application of anthropological knowledge continues to this day around anthropologists working for the U.S. Department of Defense, and contributing to the U.S. military's counter insurgency (Gonzalez 2007; Price 2007). A similar controversy has also taken place in the UK, with a research initiative entitled 'Combating Terrorism by Countering Radicalisation' launched jointly by the British Foreign and Commonwealth Office, the Economic and Social Research

Council and the Arts and Humanities Research Council (see Houtman 2006).

Such controversies point to the problematic nature of an 'applied anthropology'. From involvement in development projects, the fields of health and education and long-standing contributions in the affairs of government and policy, to more recent placements in the private sector with consumer research, the diversity of activities encompassed in this category reveals the range of the key beneficiaries of such engagement. Put slightly differently, the question that engaged anthropologists need to ask is *who* is the 'public' of a 'public anthropology'? Or for whom is such knowledge useful? This article engages with these questions around the uses and publics of anthropological research. It does not address directly all the possible fields mentioned above, to which anthropology can be said to have made important contributions. Instead, it provides some reflections on how publics have been generally conceived in the discipline and how conventions of representation may limit not only the kinds of anthropological products made but may also constrain the possibilities of dialogue with those we research. The article goes on to discuss the work of authors who have also been engaged with these themes, before providing some examples of texts that have attempted to put a 'dialogical' approach into practice.

For Thomas Eriksen in *Engaging Anthropology* (2006), the public is understood to be the general reader of anthropological books or of newspapers and magazines to which anthropologists contribute. The public is here in a sense regarded as the general public sphere of intellectual discourse. The anthropologist would then have the responsibility, given her/his insights, nuanced explanations and textured material, of contributing to various debates. This position is perhaps closer to that of Boas, in the aspiration that anthropology could provide the contribution of a true science of humanity in which all peoples are considered of equal worth, and where anthropology has a key role in mediating understanding between diverse cultures. The central argument in Eriksen's book is that anthropology is absent from the public sphere because it tends to dry out the riverbed of fieldwork experience and render its important insights unintelligible both to those we research and to the general public through use of an over-analytical language, distant from the narratives through which people make sense of their day-to-day lives. Eriksen points out that the significant public engagements of key figures in the discipline (he cites in particular Margaret Mead and Evans-Pritchard) occurred more than half a century ago and that whilst the discipline has grown significantly since this time, paradoxically its public profile has greatly diminished.

Another way to conceive of the 'public' of anthropology is through a consideration of for whom the anthropologist should be responsible. Following the controversies of U.S. anthropologists' involvement in covert intelligence gathering in the late 1960s a number of anthropologists mobilized around the Ethics Committee of the American Anthropological Association in order to provide clear statements of principles concerning the ethical responsibilities of its practitioners.

For a number of anthropologists, these responsibilities to the people we study should go beyond that of 'doing no harm', stipulated in the AAA 'Principles of Professional Responsibility', and instead ought to entail actively trying to improve the lives of those we research and their communities. In the 1950s Sol Tax coined the term 'action anthropology' to refer to a kind of anthropology that was committed to engaging with the subjects being studied in such a way as to make anthropological knowledge practically useful to their actual situation. Tax defined this activity as one in which the anthropologist has two equally valued goals: to help a group of people to solve a problem *and* to learn something in the process. The key feature of this is that not only should anthropological ethics entail not doing any harm to the people studied but also that they should not be used as means for our own ends. 'Community research is thus justifiable only to the degree that the results are imminently useful to the community and easily outweigh the disturbance to it' (Tax 1975: 515).

Tax's impetus for an action anthropology, as well as the drive of many other anthropologists for a more ethically committed discipline, largely stems from a reflection on the asymmetries of power between the anthropologists and those we study (see for instance Scheper-Hughes 1995). The so-called crisis of representation debates in the 1980s and 1990s were also concerned with these themes, challenging the possibility of a 'neutral', 'objectivist' anthropology and pointing to the field of power within which anthropological research has been historically conducted (Clifford and Marcus 1986). These critiques challenged the possibility of 'neutral' representations of culture, and pointed to the necessarily constructed and partial nature of anthropological knowledge and to the various rhetorical devices by which ethnographic texts project their authority. In response to these critiques a number of experimental approaches to the writing of ethnography were produced which sought to give more space to the voices of those researched. As James Clifford noted, in some of these experiments, such as Kevin Dwyer's (1977) dialogues, the confrontations between the anthropologist and his interlocutor come to make up a substantial part of the text. Speaking of Dwyer's and others' experiments, Clifford wrote:

> These fictions of dialogue have the effect of transforming the 'cultural' text (a ritual, an institution, a life history, or any unit of typical behaviour to be described or interpreted) into a speaking subject, who sees as well as is seen, who evades, argues, probes back. In this view of ethnography the proper referent of any account is not a represented 'world'; now it is specific instances of discourse … It locates cultural interpretation in many sorts of reciprocal contexts, and it obliges writers to find diverse ways of rendering negotiated realities as multisubjective, power-laden, and incongruent. In this view, 'culture' is always relational, an inscription of communicative processes that exist, historically, *between* subjects in relations of power. (Clifford 1986: 15)

Despite the arguments and aspirations for a 'multi-vocal' ethnography which the debates from the 1980s and 1990s put forward, such calls have tended to be theoretical with few examples of successful attempts of 'multi-vocality' being produced. Agneta Johannsen (1992), in her discussion of this period of anthropological experimentation, briefly evaluates some attempts at ethnographic dialogues, such as Dwyer's exchanges with a Moroccan Faqir (Dwyer 1977), concluding that these fail to develop a true dialogue with their interlocutors. The basis of such failures, Johannsen argues, is an asymmetry of interests and power. Johannsen also suggests that it may well be impossible to escape from the accusation that the anthropologist dominates the text. Perhaps, as she argues, the interpretive anthropologist disperses authority and lets the 'native's voice' be heard only as a means to establish their 'anti-hegemonial credentials', which in itself provides a refashioning of authority. What is important here, for the purposes of the present paper, is how such experimentation still leaves unchallenged relations of power and the conventions of academic representation. In his reflection on his own dialogues with Faqir Mbarek, Dwyer made the important observation, somewhat relating to this, of the different life projects that such interactions bring into the encounter, and perhaps to their irreconcilability (Dywer 1977).

Kirsten Hastrup also touched on this key topic when she wrote that however much we replace the monologue with dialogue, the discourse will always remain asymmetrical, for the purpose of ethnography 'is to speak *about* something for somebody; it implies contextualisation and reframing' (Hastrup 1992: 122). Whereas at the level of autobiography, the anthropologist and informant are equal, at the level of the anthropological discourse their relationship is hierarchical and the ultimate responsibility in the writing of ethnography should rest with the anthropologist. For Hastrup, anthropology, like any scientific discourse, involves a degree of violence as it makes claims to speak over and above the acts observed and heard (ibid.). In my view, Dwyer's recognition of the different life projects that anthropologists and research subjects bring into the dialogue situation is important. Equally, Hastrup's observations as to the nature of the anthropological project, in terms of its asymmetry and its symbolic violence, in relation to the project of the other, which becomes subsumed within the text, is also significant. However, I wonder if these concerns need always necessarily be evident in dialogic encounters.

Another way of approaching these challenges relates to the writing culture debate's neglect of reading texts, which involves questions of audience or publics. This theme was tackled by Talal Asad, who spoke of the notion of 'cultural translation' (Asad 1986). Anthropologists, Asad said, must 'write their people up' in the conventions of representation dictated by their discipline, by in-

stitutional life and by wider society. Cultural translation, Asad argued, needs to accommodate itself not only to a different language
– English as opposed to Kabbashi Arabic for instance – but also
to the British or North-American middle-class 'academic game',
as opposed to the 'modes of life' of the 'tribal Sudan' (Asad 1986:
159). Asad contended that, given this, translating an alien form of
life may not necessarily best be done through the representational
discourse of ethnography, but rather in some cases a dramatic performance, a dance or a piece of music may be more appropriate.
Such endeavour, Asad wrote, brings into light the wider issue of
the relationship between the anthropological work and its audience, questions of the 'uses' as opposed to the 'writings and readings' of that work. Asad asserted that as anthropologists we are
trained to translate other cultural languages as texts, translation
being essentially a matter of verbal representation (Asad 1986).
Asad here pointed to a crucial element that is often left out of debates around the 'politics of representation', mainly what he terms
the 'conventions of representation' governed by academic life and
the uses to which such products are put. It might be a fruitful
enquiry to probe how much of the concerns raised by Johannsen,
Hastrup and Dwyer above stem from such conventions.[1] Perhaps
such discussions only occur at the fringes of the discipline, where
the challenges to the 'rules of the game' are not so strongly felt. At
the same time, to engage directly with such conventions requires
forms of creative experimentation and praxis, which perhaps by
definition can only occur in the space of the margins.[2]

An author who has addressed how a dialogical approach might
unfold through text is Agneta Johannsen. Combining the contributions of applied anthropology with what she identifies as the
insights of a postmodern, interpretative ethnography, Johannsen
suggested what she calls a postmodern applied anthropology.
Johannsen's project entails neither seeking to solve problems, as
Tax's action anthropology proposed, nor representing a 'target'
culture as interpretive anthropologists attempt to do. Rather: 'The
post-modernist applied anthropologist can provide a mechanism
by which the target community represents itself and determines
the nature and solution of its problem' (Johannsen 1992: 72).

Johannsen took interpretative anthropology's self-critical concern with ethical responsibilities in the representation of a culture and combined these with applied anthropology's motivation to work *with* particular communities. Interpretative ethnographies though, are also concerned with the epistemological difficulties in the representation of ethnographic data. A further motivation of such an applied postmodern ethnography for Johannsen is that these difficulties of representation are faced through establishing a dialogue in which the anthropologist 'seeks to present objectively and fruitfully a number of different 'voices', each of which has the authority to contribute a thorough portrayal of the target culture meaningful to a variety of readerships' (Johannsen 1992: 74). For Johannsen such an ethnography based on dialogue becomes a source for both scholars and 'natives', as well as potentially a broader public, challenging a convention in anthropology of writing principally for academics.

Such a proposal raises a number of questions and challenges to traditional ways of conducting fieldwork and of producing ethnographies. Johannsen proposed some interesting points of convergence of an applied anthropology that is primarily responsible to the people it studies with the concerns of interpretive anthropology and its critique of scholarly and scientific authority and of the difficulties surrounding cultural representation. Unfortunately, Johannsen's paper did not provide examples of what such a proposal would look like in practice. In the next section I will provide a brief exposition of some endeavours that may be classified as dialogical in their approach.

Cabeça de Porco

An example of what such a dialogic anthropology could look like in text is the best-selling Brazilian book *Cabeça de Porco* [*Pig's Head*] (2005), written collaboratively by the anthropologist Luiz Eduardo Soares, the rapper MV Bill and his Hip Hop producer Celso Athayde. The book addresses the issue of the growth of drug trafficking gangs across Brazil and their increasing power in urban shanty-towns [*favelas*] where they have, over the last twenty years, come to be part of the day-to-day lives of many of these communities. More specifically the book addresses the increasing numbers of young recruits joining these gangs, outlining how working in the gang has become for many an attractive option in an environment of increasing inequality, unemployment and in a consumerist society whose desirable products are out of reach for many. Further, the book tackles the repressive and violent responses of the state to these gangs, whose actions within the *favelas* has often served to antagonise residents and further encourage young people to join the gangs as a way of seeking protection and retaliation. The book explores these issues, as well as the broader social context in which *favela* residents, especially its black youth, are discriminated against and denied opportunities for social mobility.

Though such issues have been tackled by anthropologists before (see Zaluar 1994; Vianna 1997; De Assis 1999; Dowdney 2002) the novelty of the book and what makes it dialogical lies in how it was produced and received. The book merged the ethnographic work and personal experiences of Soares with research carried out by Bill and Athayde. The latter two, residents of one of Rio's largest *favelas*, Cidade de Deus [City of God], carried out research, with no formal training, over a number of years all over Brazil with young people involved in drug trafficking gangs. The important thing here is that, through this research, MV Bill and Celso Athayde were reflecting upon experiences that were part of their day-to-day lives in Cidade de Deus and other *favelas*. The critical culture in which both are involved is not that of academia but of Hip Hop. The manifestation of this culture in Brazil, though diverse, tends to be more akin to the early politicized Hip Hop from New York, with messages about black empowerment and the need to be aware of one's history and to 'fight the power', than to the Hip Hop that glamourizes consumerism, which is more commonly found through the mass-media across the globe.

Cabeça de Porco alternates in its narrative between texts written separately by the three writers. Bill and Athayde provided more personal accounts of their encounters with young people across a number of *favelas* throughout the country alongside their personal experiences of growing up and living in these communities.

Soares, though also using an engaging and accessible language, provided a more theoretical analysis of the causes of urban crime, of the expansion of the drug trade, of the responses of the state, and of the origins and perpetuation of social stigma towards young, black, *favela* residents. The balance between interesting and captivating stories written in a clear and easily understood language, combined with nuanced, theoretically rich, but jargon-free analysis of these themes accounts for the success of the book. The book addressed important questions for many urban dwellers in Brazil, the issue of security, drug gangs, violence, youth, poverty and discrimination. Sales of the book and reviews show how well it was received, even though its key messages were not uncontroversial: of the need for a systemic and humanizing understanding of why young people join the drug gangs; of the police's collusion in the drug trade and the violence it perpetuates against these communities, as well the failure of the government and society more generally to tackle the problem adequately. The book topped the best-seller's list in Brazil for many weeks and, perhaps more interestingly, served to catalyse a number of reading groups of young people in a number of *favelas* throughout Brazil. The book has since been read right across Brazilian society.

The dialogical element of this project is clear. This is most succinctly described by Fernanda Abreu, a Brazilian musician, who wrote a review for the cover of the book, referring to the partnership between the *favela* and the asphalt (the region where middle-class non-*favela* residents live):

A connection white middle-class asphalt + black poor peripheric. Two worlds that do not communicate. But here, despite the distance that separates them, what surprises are the similarities and not the differences. A possible partnership? Two worlds. One legitimating the other. (Fernanda Abreu in Soares, Bill and Athayde 2005, my translation)

The success of the project lies in its complementarity. Two perspectives are given, one more experience-near but no less analytical, the other able to link across diverse areas and theories of social analysis and meaningfully integrate these experiences, as well those of Soares himself, into a satisfying whole. At the same time the 'authority' of the text is derived, as Abreu states above, from a mutual acknowledgement of the value of each other's perspective around the phenomena of young people who are part of drug-trafficking gangs. This is slightly different from what Johannsen proposed, in an applied postmodern anthropology. For here it is not about giving the people studied the means of representation and letting them get on with it. Rather, it is about a dialogue, in this case through the text, of complementary perspectives.

Nós: The Revolution of the Day to Day

A second, more humble example is from recent work in which I was involved in Rio de Janeiro with young people who participate in a variety of social movements, community development and non-governmental organizations in the city (Butler and Prince-swal 2008). The project *Cultures of Participation* began in May 2005, with the objective of understanding how young people perceive and practice citizenship in the public sphere in the city of Rio de Janeiro and what concepts such as 'citizenship' and 'partici-pation' mean to them.[3] Initially we identified 20 different initia-tives working with this sector of the population, and focusing on social justice, community development, citizenship and access to cultural opportunities. These initiatives included community organizations, NGOs, a union, the landless movement as well as more informal groups such as Hip Hop activists. Following visits and interviews with coordinators and young people participating in these organizations, we began a second stage where we sought to deepen the stories of engagement and participation of a diverse group of youths. The idea was to go beyond the interviews with young people and initiate a collective process of narration and debate about their experiences. As the participants in this phase themselves described, it was a process of reflection about 'their lives inside activism and activism inside their lives', and the chal-lenges, difficulties and pleasures of their chosen paths.

Over a period of nine months a group of seven young people between the ages of 15 and 27, active in diverse groups in the city's public sphere, met with members of the research team to develop narratives about their experiences of participation and what this has meant for them. The result of this process of individual and collective creation is a publication designed by the group containing the narratives they themselves wrote. The book *Nós: A Revolução de Cada Dia* [*Nós: The Revolution of the Day to Day*] (2007) presents the trajectories of these young people, focusing on their participation in different groups, movements and projects engaged in a struggle for citizenship and social justice.[4]

For example, Quênia, a 23-year old woman, has been involved in a number of community arts projects and a rap group and has been engaged in questions around black women's self-esteem. In her chapter, as in those of the other young people, she narrated the intricate connections between the personal and the political, reflecting on everyday experiences of discrimination as well as on the processes through which she became engaged in movements trying to combat the many forms this takes:

> During pre-school days, if I remember rightly, we were only two black girls in the classroom – something that has not changed much [in the south of Brazil]. All the teachers were white. On TV all the presenters were white. So what would my reference of beauty be??? It is complicated only having one reference of the beautiful in a stage where you are creating your identity. You are making friends, making up your group in which 'we are all equal', we have 'the same toys', the same white dolls. Yes, but the same as my white friends. And this difference I only noticed when my mum arrived with a black doll. You can say that at that moment I was very shocked: 'What do you mean???' 'Who told her that I wanted to be different?' 'And who told her that I wanted a BLACK doll??' Not to say, curly hair. That doll called Luana was for me the last straw. How different would I be from my friends who had Xuxa?[5] No one knew who Luana was! I didn't know and didn't care. This understanding of what it is to be the same and what it is to be different I only came to acquire over the years. (Quênia Lopes in *Nós* 2007: 35)

These themes of being the same yet different, of the multiplicity of sites of the 'political' and how young people come to be gradually aware of such issues and engage in action towards social change through a number of different forms and spaces, runs through all of the texts in the book. At the same time these points resonate with the themes that the research project as a whole was trying to explore. In Quênia's case, her process of political awakening came through her encounter with Hip Hop culture:

> When I started going to break-dance circles, I saw happy black people, saw aware black people. It was a movement of self-affirmation, and I was very happy to be part of this movement of liberation that was, mainly, freeing my mind. This shock of awareness changed my life. In less than four months me and my friends already had a rap group made up only of black women, with the name of Anastácias because it identified us with the life-story of this warrior woman. With this group we won national prizes in music, with our work being recognised in the media throughout the country. (*Nós* 2007: 36)

In the research team we wanted to go beyond our analysis of these themes and have young people's own reflections on the matter, not just through interviews or debates but through a collectively constructed research product that could speak to not only other researchers but also to other young people. Centred on the theme of 'participation', we wanted to try to practice what we were investigating, incorporating at least one element of the research as a participative experiment. Though we were the catalysts for the process and provided its resources, we were at least willing to explore in practice those 'conventions of representation' through a joint product, whose basis was their own texts. This has subsequently been used and disseminated by its authors as they see fit. At the same time, the research team was acutely mindful of the relations of power inherent in such an endeavour and tried to be as transparent about these as possible whenever they came to light.

Both the research team and the research participants believe that the experiment was on the whole successful. The authors each wrote a short text at the end of the book outlining their reflections on the process of making the publication. Here is what Manuelle Rosa, who is in her early twenties and active in community journalism, wrote about her experience:

> Before being invited to participate in this project, I had never had time to think about this thing called Participation. Deep

down I knew that my work brought something good for me and for others, but I had not perceived its real function. It was through the conversations with other participants and the writing of my own trajectory that I could reflect about what I do, of the importance that this has for me, and the repercussions of this in the place where I live.

After a long period without having a clue what to write, and after many rough drafts thrown in the bin, I got to the final text with some questions and answers that had never occurred to me before. In truth, this text is not finished, and I don't even know if it will be one day, because many of the questions that emerged during this process still have no answer. But I arrive here with the certainty that the experience I had was worth it. It was really good to stop for a moment from the rush of daily work and look at what I have been doing. And I liked what I saw. As for the answers, I am still looking for them. (*Nós* 2007: 65)

Though challenging and very different from the solitary analysis that most anthropologists engage in post-fieldwork, working in collaboration allowed for not only the creation of a group of rich, experience-near yet reflexive personal accounts of young people's engagement in public action initiatives, but also encouraged a learning process by all involved, as Manuelle articulates above. For the young people, the context of this collaborative work offered the opportunity to debate and exchange with others from different groups and areas of public action. This exchange allowed for mutual reflection upon common themes and challenges. The writing process, though not easy for everyone, also provoked reflection on key concepts, such as that of 'participation' that had not been fully considered before.[6]

For us in the research team the experience was also unsettling, for through this encounter we came to reflect upon our own practices as researchers and our commitment (or lack thereof) to processes of social transformation. Working with groups of young people who were clearly committed to different forms of combating injustice on various fronts provoked us to question our own activities, our own participation as well as the limitations of our role as 'researcher'.

Discussion

This example from our research and that found in the book *Cabeça de Porco* offer some illustrations of attempts at a text-based dialogic anthropology. Clearly, initiatives such as these also have a number of shortcomings. One challenge such an approach faces is that if collaborations are to be based through the medium of the written word, research participants may not be equipped with the levels of literacy required to represent their own experiences and reflections faithfully through text. One challenge we faced in our project was the fine line between acting as editors, making sure the narratives of the young people were clearly understood and reflected what they really wanted to say, and not wishing to impose our own writing styles and conventions on their mode of expression. A way to overcome these challenges may well be to opt for other forms of collaboration that are not text-based.

There are of course a number of other more serious difficulties with such an approach. As with the difficulties in anthropological research more generally, with the goal of seeking to represent 'culture', how representative any accounts of a particular community or groups of people are will always be open to question. Such a dialogical approach may only be practical with a relatively small number of people. In the examples mentioned here, there were frequently only a handful of research participants involved. The difficulty is then how to select such participants. In the case of our work in Rio de Janeiro, such selection emerged only after a period of fieldwork through which we identified a range of initiatives and organizations in which young people took part. After identifying young people who appeared to be more engaged in these organizations, we sought a diversity of areas of activity.

The second challenge in such an approach is the actual dialogical process itself. In the case of our work, this entailed nine months of periodical meetings with debates, and a number of drafts of the texts, which the group circulated to the research team and amongst themselves. Catalysing such a process may not be appealing to many researchers, requiring different sets of skills and different time-scales. Here, again, we have much to learn from

Freirean pedagogical approaches as well as other participatory research practices (Freire 1976, [1970] 1993).

A third challenge concerns its appropriateness. As mentioned, working in this way is not necessarily suitable or desirable in all cases. The examples given here involved people with an aspiration to working together on a joint product. Though clearly researchers and those involved in these projects may well have, as Dwyer reflected, different life projects, motivations, worldviews and so forth, these products or encounters show that there is also room for at least a partial overlap or a willingness to work together. Were such willingness not to be found, it would not be possible or desirable to pursue such an endeavour. What is important from these dialogues is the sense of mutual learning and respect, and how through embodying different 'projects' (of worldview, ethics, epistemology, ontology) the participants in many ways learn about how much they share in common.

Concluding Remarks

Before concluding that the most important reason why anthropology does not occupy its rightful role in the public sphere is due to its impenetrable language, Eriksen considers what he calls the many 'scapegoats' for anthropologists' reluctance to engage with the public. These include the bureaucratization of academic life leading to less time to engage with society more broadly; the increasing specialization of academics to the point of fragmentation; the diminishing of their societal authority. Though I do not disagree that the issue of language and of offering more engaging narratives is an important one for anthropologists to have a greater public presence, I also believe that these so-called 'scapegoats' may well be the most important reasons for anthropologists' reluctance to engage in dialogue. The dialogic products I have been referring to here have in some way challenged the conventions of representations. However, I am not arguing that such experiments should replace ethnographic writing which, as Hastrup convincingly argued, is primarily speaking *about* something for somebody and implies contextualisation and reframing. Neither, clearly, is this paper arguing that we cease considering our colleagues as the main public for our writing. Instead this article has shown how, on top of these activities, much is to be gained from speaking with and alongside those with whom we work. Moreover, this speaking with requires us to enquire deeply into what have been referred to here as the conventions of representation and how these are maintained by particular academic cultures and logic. A dialogical anthropology should not shy away from self-reflection and an examination of the conditions of the production of knowledge, nor should it lead to paralysis of doing research. Instead it could lead to creative ways of interacting with those we work with as we jointly engage with the important questions of our times.

Notes

1. This point has also been briefly tackled by George Marcus who speaks of how such conventions of representation seem to be learned and shaped by the requirements of the monograph writing for a PhD, which provides a model and which, many would argue, provides an antiquated standard and practice for research and writing (Marcus 1986: 263).

2. Though falling outside the core theme of this paper, it is important to mention that such debates appear to have a more central place in the subfields of visual anthropology and museum ethnography. Here as early as the 1960s and 1970s ethnographic filmmakers like Jean Rouch and David and Judith MacDougall faced similar problems of how to create filmic texts which were more dialogical and true to the process that went into their making. Initially opting for an approach that portrayed in their films the process of its construction, such as Rouch's *Chronique d'un été* (1961) and the MacDougalls' *The Wedding Camels* (1977), these ethnographic filmmakers went on to collaborate more directly with those depicted. In a so-called 'participatory cinema' such as Rouch's *Jaguar* (1967) or MacDougall's *Goodbye Old Man* (1977) the collaboration between filmmakers and the film subjects (West Africans in the case of the former and Australian Aboriginals in the later) becomes a guiding principle of the film (see for instance MacDougall 1998). Added to such developments in visual anthropology, in the 1980s and 1990s we also see the emergence of what Faye Ginsburg has

termed 'indigenous media'. Here, at times emerging out of collaborations with anthropologists, this phenomenon has entailed the use of
new communication media by indigenous communities themselves.
The most famous early examples of this include the use of video by
the Kayapo (Turner 1992), Australian Aboriginals (Ginsburg 1991), as
well as by Inuit communities. I have only briefly mentioned these collaborative or even dialogical experiments through audio-visual media
here to point out that such concerns have been occurring in sub-fields
of the discipline and that these examples and the reflections they have
generated could similarly contribute to dialogic approaches through
the text.

3. The project was carried out with the Brazilian action-research NGO
   CIESPI (the International Center for Research and Policy on Childhood); other members of the team included Marcelo Princeswal
   and Roberta Abreu. This research was funded by the UK Economic
   and Social Research Council's Non-Governmental and Public Action
   Programme, which is a multi-disciplinary international research programme designed to investigate the variety of ways through which
   people in different countries organize together to bring about social
   change (see www.lse.ac.uk/collections/NGPA/).
4. Translated as *Nós: The Revolution of the Day to Day,* an electronic version of the book is available at: <http://ciespi.org.br/english/projetos_
   culturas.htm> or <http://www.lse.ac.uk/collections/NGPA/Research_
   projects/butler.htm#id2527269>.
5. Xuxa, a very famous Brazilian children's TV presenter with a range of
   products for children, is white, with blue eyes and blonde hair.
6. It must be admitted that the term 'participation' is itself problematic
   (see for instance Rahnema 1992; Cooke and Kothari 2004). Significantly, local terms such as 'solidarity' were more important in the conversations with young people to represent values and the justification
   for forms of engagement in public action they felt to be meaningful.
   Though key terms are important, more significant are the set of practices, meanings, feelings, identities and relationships that are reflected
   upon and for which key terms only provide an initial framing.

References

AAA 'Principles of Professional Responsibility' [1971] (1986) <http://
www.aaanet.org/stmts/ethstmnt.htm> (accessed 7 June 2007).

Asad, T. (1986), 'The Concept of Cultural Translation in British Social
Anthropology', in *Writing Culture: The Poetics and Politics of Ethnogra-*

phy, (eds.) J. Clifford and G. Marcus (Berkley: University of California Press).

Asad, T. (ed.) (1973), *Anthropology and the Colonial Encounter* (New York: Humanities Press).

Butler, U. and Princeswal, M. (2008), 'Cultures of Participation: Young People's Engagement in the Public Sphere in Brazil', (NGPA Working Papers Series, London School of Economics: London).

CIESPI (2007), *Nós: A Revolução de Cada Dia* (Rio de Janeiro: CIESPI/ PUC).

Clifford, J. (1986), 'Introduction: Partial Truths', in *Writing Culture: The Poetics and Politics of Ethnography*, (eds.) J. Clifford and G. Marcus (Berkley: University of California Press).

Clifford, J. and Marcus, G. (eds.) (1986), *Writing Culture: The Poetics and Politics of Ethnography* (Berkley: University of California Press).

Cooke, B. and Kothari, U. (eds.) (2004), *Participation: The New Tyranny?* (London: Zed Books).

De Assis, S. G. (1999), *Traçando Caminhos em uma Sociedade Violenta: A vida de jovens infratores e de seus irmãos não-infratores* (Rio de Janeiro: Fundação Oswaldo Cruz).

Dowdney, L. (2002), 'Child Combatants in Organized Armed Violence: A Study of Children and Adolescents Involved in Territorial Drug Faction Disputes in Rio de Janeiro' (Rio de Janeiro: ISER/Viva Rio).

Dwyer, K. (1977), 'On the Dialogic Of Fieldwork', *Dialectical Anthropology* 2, 143–151.

Eriksen, T. H. (2006), *Engaging Anthropology: The Case for a Public Presence* (Oxford: Berg).

Freire, P. (1976), *Ação Cultural Para Liberdade* (Rio de Janeiro: Editora Paz e Terra).

Freire, P. [1970] (1993), *Pedagogy of the Oppressed* (London: Penguin Press).

Gardner, K. and Lewis, D. (1996), *Anthropology, Development and the Postmodern Challenge* (London: Pluto Press).

Ginsburg, F. (1991), 'Indigenous Media: Faustian Contract or Global Village', *Cultural Anthropology* 6, no. 1: 92–112.

González, R. (2007), 'Towards Mercenary Anthropology? The New US Army Counterinsurgency Manual *FM 3–24* and the Military-anthropology Complex', *Anthropology Today* 23, no. 3: 14–20.

González, R. (ed.) (2004), *Anthropology in the Public Sphere: Speaking out on War, Peace and American Power* (Austin: University of Texas Press).

Hastrup, K. (1992) 'Writing Ethnography: State of the Art', in *Anthropology and Autobiography*. Okely, Judith and Callaway, Helen (Eds). (London: Routledge).

Houtman, G. (2006), 'Double or quits', *Anthropology Today* 22, n.6: 1–3.

Johannsen, A. (1992), 'Applied Anthropology and Post-Modernist Ethnography', *Human Organization* 51, no. 1: 71–81.

MacDougall, D. (1998), *Transcultural Cinema* (Princeton: Princeton University Press).

Marcus, G. (1986) 'Afterword: Ethnographic Writing and Anthropological Careers', in *Writing Culture: The Poetics and Politics of Ethnography,* (eds.) Clifford, James and Marcus, George, (Berkley: University of California Press).

Price, D. (2007), 'Buying a piece of anthropology, Part 1: Human Ecology and unwitting anthropological research for the CIA', *Anthropology Today* 23, no. 3: 8–14.

Rahnema, M. (1992), 'Participation', in *The Development Dictionary. A Guide to Knowledge as Power,* Wolfgan Sachs (ed.), (London: Zed Books Ltd).

Scheper-Hughes, N. (1995), 'The Primacy of the Ethical: Propositions for a Militant Anthropology', *Current Anthropology* 36, no. 3: 409–420.

Soares, L. E., Bill, MV and Athayde, C. (2005), *Cabeça de Porco* (Rio de Janeiro: Editora Objetiva).

Tax, S. (1975), 'Action Anthropology', *Current Anthropology* 16, no. 4: 514–517.

Vianna, H. (ed.) (1997), *Galeras Cariocas: territórios de conflitos e encontros culturais* (Rio de Janeiro: Editora UFRJ).

Wolf, E. and Jorgensen, J. (1970), 'Anthropology on the Warpath in Thailand', *New York Review of Books* 15, no. 9: 26–35.

Zaluar, A. (1994), 'Gangsters and Remote-control Juvenile Delinquents: Youth and Crime', in *Children in Brazil Today: A Challenge for the Third Millennium,* (ed.) I. Rizzini (Rio de Janeiro: Editora Universitária Santa Ursula).

Films

MacDougall, D. and MacDougall, J. (dir.) (1977), *The Wedding Camels* (California: University of California Extension Center for Media).

——— (1977), *Goodbye Old Man* (California: University of California Extension Center for Media).

Rouch, J. (dir) (1960), *Chronique de une Eté* (France: CNRS).

——— (1957–1967), *Jaguar* (France: Films de la Pléiade).

Mapping Solidarity
How Public Anthropology Provides Guidelines for Advocacy Networks

Raúl Acosta

Introduction

On the morning of 25 October 2004, a meeting in the city of Cana-rana, in the southern frontier zone of the Brazilian Amazon, started with the projection of an image of the earth rotating as if seen from outer space. As it moved, the image gradually zoomed into Brazil, then the Amazon region, then the state of Mato Grosso, and froze in the Xingu River basin. This happened while a speaker said the opening words of the gathering that brought together over three hundred representatives of groups either based in the area or interested in its environment. It was the first time that local small farmers sat at the same negotiating table as industrial soy produc-ers. This meeting was convened by a team of non-governmental organizations (NGOs) led by Instituto Socioambiental (ISA 2009). Its purpose was to form a network with all those in attendance to start a campaign to protect and restore the springs that feed the Xingu River, a tributary of the Amazon. The problems that have affected these springs range from drying up due to deforestation to increasing levels of pollution caused by industrial farming. Among those involved were several indigenous communities whose protected territories either lie in the basin of the Xingu or are crossed by the river, like the Xingu Indigenous Park, a pro-tected area for 16 ethnic groups (Schwartzman and Zimmerman

2005). The name for the network and campaign chosen by vote in the general assembly was 'Y Ikatu Xingu, which means 'Save the good water of the Xingu River' in the Tupi language. There were also scientists and government officials who had never before sat in such a diverse congregation. An indigenous leader seemed to reproach this panel of white middle-aged men from government, NGOs and other institutions: 'We indigenous peoples always waited for you to call us to start a dialogue, but as indigenous people we are considered a minority, as if we were animals. We are human beings, and need respect' (field notes 2004). He nevertheless used a nationalist discourse to call for a joint effort to save the river, 'because it's not only the Xingu [river] that is dying, it's the whole of Brazil.'

After three days of debates and presentations, the meeting ended with a series of specific tasks distributed among many of those attending. A committee was formed to coordinate activities and inform any news to all other network members. The meeting's conclusions and plans seemed to be a roadmap for the collective effort to protect and restore the river's springs. Other maps, physical ones, were an important part of the gathering. The main one distributed to all those attending was of the whole basin, based on a satellite photograph digitally manipulated to highlight in different colours areas that have long been deforested, have recently been deforested, are protected, have been re-forested or maintain their original vegetation. This map clearly showed the threats that pose a risk for the future of the river and, therefore, for the area's environment. It was the key to the meeting's success, as it was designed to be easy to understand and very informative of the situation. The map was therefore the backbone of the network. Its use of data from different research approaches mirrored ISA's multidisciplinary character. It is an NGO that has mainly focused its efforts on improving living conditions for indigenous communities in Brazil since its foundation in 1994. It inherited experience, documents and staff from two organizations that had already been working on indigenous rights for fifteen years in Brazil. Anthropologists have been the backbone of the NGO since its inception. This fact has allowed it to bridge cultural differences in sensitive issues. All this is summarized in ISA's map, accessible to a wide variety of stakeholders, with their respective priorities and interests, and yet with a clear common goal of protecting river springs.

This paper puts forward the idea that public anthropologists can provide comprehensible maps for political action of advocacy networks. This idea stems from examples such as that described above, which entail 'public conversations with anthropological insight' (Borofsky 2007). This requires that the analyses and deductions stemming from anthropological observations provide an understanding of the complexities of dialogues, linkages and relations across cultural practices, histories and contexts. In their political aspirations, advocacy networks strive to bridge a wide array of identities and localities in order to advocate for a common cause. These types of efforts inevitably lead to ongoing friction (Tsing 2005) that can in turn mean clashing projects or ideals, not only between those involved in networks but also between them and governments or other institutional actors.

This paper does not seek to imply that the referred network was 'successful', but rather that it has remained a sustained association for several years. Its long-term campaign does not rely on a 'social construction' of success like that of the development projects Mosse (2005) described in his ethnography of British aid in India. The difference lies in the fact that while official projects like those of the Department for International Development (DfID), which Mosse described, rely on short-term evaluations of achieved goals in order to be allowed to continue by a central office, while projects of an advocacy network such as 'Y Ikatu Xingu rely more on an ongoing maintenance of their legitimacy to all stakeholders involved. In order to achieve this, the organizations convening 'Y Ikatu Xingu stated a clear timeline over a long period of time for the various actions to achieve the campaign's goal of protecting springs and improving the water quality of the tributaries that feed the Xingu River. These include scientific studies of pollution, establishing protected areas and training enough people to oversee the efforts to allow for ongoing protection and improvement. It is a scheme that allows everyone involved to understand the campaign's long-term logic. During that time, the network motivates its members with reports, workshops, information and events.

Some of the activities are even celebratory, thus offering a renewed sense of intertwined purposes between the campaign and life in the area. A good example is the commemoration of the World Environment Day, for which in 2009 the network sponsored a series of sporting and recreational activities, as well as a music concert and a reception in the city of Canarana, where the network started. These many actions ensure a continuity of the association and its purpose, even if it changes in some of its aspects. A key ingredient that has allowed the survival of the network is the mediation work by anthropologists which has helped bridge cultural differences through research, documents or insights, which will be explained further below. The practice of public anthropology in this scenario is applied to the mediation between contrasting understandings of the relation between social life and its natural environment. This hands-on approach, it is proposed here, can provide guidelines or maps to help advocacy networks navigate through difficult terrains full of misunderstandings and conflict.

In order to make the case stated above, I divide this paper into two parts. The first one is a brief description of the advocacy network portrayed above in the Brazilian Amazon. It provides further details of meetings in which mediation skills within such webs were challenged by a diversity of cultural understandings, practical responses and intellectual approaches among their members. The second part is a reflection on the complex interconnections that are of increasing interest to anthropologists. It is a general discussion on advocacy networks as a transnational version of social solidarity and of the involvement of anthropologists both within such networks and outside of them as researchers. In a milieu where some academic production is readily available to activists and NGO workers, it is appropriate to reflect on such research and its consequences. Before exploring the web portrayed, the following paragraph provides further clarification about the type of associations advocacy networks entail.

Keck and Sikkink (1998) described trans-national advocacy networks as webs that link social movements, non-governmental organizations (NGOs), epistemic communities, alternative media, individuals and other organizations. Keck and Sikkink defined these groupings as networks of 'relevant actors working internationally on an issue, who are bound together by shared values, a common discourse, and dense exchange of information and services' (1998: 2). They are becoming indispensable legitimacy providers in all scales of power structures. This has come about rather swiftly, a reason why most of them are innovating as they carry out their campaigns and activities. Their influence in the more institutional political arena comes from a reliance on their own flexibility and expertise. It is also related, however, to their organizing principle of collective decision-making in tune with the governance concept stressed by the World Bank and other aid agencies over the last couple of decades. Anthropologists have recently criticized some of these networks by dissecting their inner workings in thorough ethnographies. For example, Riles (2000) focused on aesthetic qualities of document production in Pacific networks of women's rights, which had an effect on how their work was used once completed (usually filed away). Mosse (2005) looked at development projects from within an aid agency, trying thus to understand why some projects simply do not achieve their aims. These examples, among others, show how anthropological research can deconstruct realities that are covered with politically correct language. These are academic approaches to hands-on associations. The argument in this paper relates mainly to hands-on anthropologists in such associations, who usually read and translate analyses from others into the ongoing deliberations and negotiations they facilitate. This combination, therefore, makes it possible for researchers to put forward principles that can serve as guidelines for these new political organizations.

Networks Flow

The research project on which this paper is based set out to observe two sets of advocacy networks, one in the Amazon and another one in the Mediterranean (Acosta 2007). The purpose was to study the political practice involved in them as an innovative way to engage in public issues. The study used a network model, which provides a useful focus to understand power relations that challenge established institutions. After analyzing the political practice of the networks, the role of anthropologists within their fluid structures became clear. This part of the paper is dedicated to an ethnographic description of one advocacy network in the Amazon, as it comprises several characteristics that are relevant to this analysis. The names of the main NGOs portrayed here will be their real ones, but their members and the activists involved have been changed, to guard their anonymity.

The meeting described at the start of this paper showed the advantage of having anthropologists as mediators between different groups. ISA, the leading NGO in charge of the campaign, clarifies in its webpage that this project started because since the mid-1990s leaders of the Xingu Indigenous Park complained about the negative effects the Xingu River was experiencing due to deforestation and farming ('Y Ikatu Xingu 2007). After years of ongoing projects and dialogues, its members decided to combine different types of information into maps, which were central for an effective socio-environmental campaign with a clear message. This effort paid off as all groups involved have shown their ongoing commitment to the plan, with wide support from many parts of the country. Several companies have awarded the project a series of grants and support of different sorts. In January 2006, HSBC awarded the campaign an award for environmental protection. By bringing so many different institutional and individual actors together and managing to organize activities in stages and with clear responsibilities and commitments, the leading team helped earn the support and sponsorship from different government agencies.

All this, however, did not mean that the negotiations ran smoothly. There were tensions among those attending for many reasons. One was between small family farmers and large industrial ones, as the former claimed to be forced into selling their land or crops at low prices to the latter, who have the resources, experience and connections to transport and commercialize the grains to markets worldwide. Another source of conflict is between the new-arrivals versus those who have been in the area for longer. One of the key clashes, however, which always grabs the attention of researchers and journalists, is the one between indigenous groups and the populations around them. The speech quoted in the introduction summarized the majority view of the indigenous groups attending to the meeting at Canarana. In fact, at the end of the meeting a group of Kaiabi held a war dance to show their concern about its potential outcomes; as one member of the group later told me: 'It's not the first time they tell us that everything will improve'. The ongoing negotiations were full of ongoing misunderstandings due to prejudice and lack of empathy. For example, one member of a large agribusiness company seeking to lease land from the protected areas destined to indigenous populations complained to me in private about their unwillingness to lease it. 'With only a few thousand hectares producing soy, all the community could make enough money to retire comfortably to Florida', he said with a wry smile. All these conflicts, however, helped legitimize the meeting as each was addressed directly by the organizers. This open and direct effort to leave their historical mutual conflicts to one side and focus on a common goal has allowed the campaign to remain an ongoing project with collective support and a stated long-term agenda.

Another NGO that was part of the organizing team was IPAM, or Instituto de Pesquisa Ambiental da Amazônia. This is an NGO focused on scientific research, the results of which they use to 'contribute to the development process in Amazonia' (IPAM 2006). It has around 130 paid employees, plus students and volunteers who take part in experiments and studies. One of the founders and leading scientists of IPAM told me in an interview that the organization's aim is to level the playing field between all stakeholders involved in the area to achieve fruitful negotiations that make a difference. Most of the organization's projects are systematic studies of environmental matters, such as the study of effects of diminishing rainfall or fire in a primary forest area. They link these studies with social projects that aim to seek collective solutions to problems that affect all stakeholders. The detailed information they produce, along with their conclusions and proposals, are therefore shared with communities, producers and government. They take part in advocacy networks, usually in a leading or mediating role, alongside small farmers' unions, large agribusinesses, indigenous groups, other NGOs, students and other stakeholders. The overall aim of their participation in campaigns such as 'Y Ikatu Xingu is to achieve a better governance model in the area. During my observation period, at least two of IPAM's researchers were anthropologists, whose inquiries directly concerned contrasting uses of forest goods and plants in the area. Their anthropological insights were therefore used along with other information for reports. What they provided that added value was a map of cultural reactions to particular problems of the area. This in turn helped the NGO design the way its members shared their analyses in order to reach potential solutions that would not alienate any of the stakeholders. The legitimacy that IPAM earned in governmental, academic or business sectors due to their peer-reviewed publications was not enough to help them be heard by union members or small farmers. 'We need to be sensitive to how people understand scientific data', one of the researchers told me after a problematic meeting in Santarém.

Both IPAM and ISA were skilled mediators between all stakeholders, who came together in Canarana for the inaugural meeting of the '*Y Ikatu Xingu* campaign. ISA's history and current work is informed by anthropological studies of the diversity among Brazil's indigenous populations, and their relation to the natural environment. IPAM is focused on a natural-scientific study of the Amazon, but always with an acute awareness of the need to translate their results into a clear discourse with images that allow all stakeholders to understand them and their implications. The endeavour of both NGOs as conveners of the network thus represented an effort to achieve a dialogue between all sides interested in the issue at hand (the protection of the springs). The main tool they used, a map with descriptive layers pointing to several waves of deforestation, helped everyone understand how quickly the area had degraded, thus inviting the sceptical groups to become involved. Members of both organizations talked about the situation with care not to exert any type of pressure on others, but rather explain plainly what is happening, and what would change if everyone in the area were involved in protecting the springs. This strategy proved useful because everyone was witness to the quick transformation of the area. The city where the meeting took place, Canarana, in the state of Mato Grosso, had only existed for a few decades. It was created in the 1970s as a colonizing project organized by a Southern protestant pastor to cultivate the land in the region, using a North American model of urbanization and land use. In four decades, the area surrounding the city changed from a thick forest to mainly soy producing fields. Migration to the region, especially from the south of Brazil, has been the main force behind the increasing agriculture and cattle ranching (Lisansky 1990).

A key population in the area are the fourteen ethnic groups that live in the Xingu national park. The long experience of ISA personnel in the area endows them with legitimacy to help local communities and to mediate their dialogues with other groups. One of ISA's members' father was among the founders of the park in 1961. This focus has been at the core of ISA. Several of its anthropologists work for long periods of time within the communities in the park. Other non-anthropologist personnel have acquired a type of anthropological sensitivity towards cultural diversity in order to carry out their work for ISA. As an NGO focused on socio-environmental issues, however, it has framed its focus within environmental perspectives. It has published studies of urbanization, environmental hazards, conservation areas, indigenous rights and diversity, among many others. I believe that its expertise in anthropology within a socio-environmental frame has allowed it to bridge cultural understandings of development and wellbeing, as well as of environment and social life. Having IPAM as a close associate has allowed both organizations to gain experience in this line and benefit from the production of scientific experiments. These elements have allowed them to communicate successfully the common benefits of working together in the 'Y Ikatu Xingu campaign.

Anthropological Perspectives on Interconnections

Anna Tsing (2005: 4) referred to friction in terms of a stress caused by cultural interaction, as 'the awkward, unequal, unstable, and creative qualities of interconnection across difference'. Cultures, however contentious the concept may be, are continuously co-produced by this process, she argued. Networks do not hold any kind of cultural unity, nor do they entail cultural reifications. They do suffer from friction produced by difference. Rather than trying to homogenize a type of identity, members of the network described above are involved in efforts to engage social and political diversity in order to reach a unified solution to a common problem. This characteristic makes them a privileged type of association for anthropologists to observe interactions across difference. This capacity is particularly relevant in the current historical moment, due to the increased infrastructure that allows for ongoing densification of interconnections in various public spheres. Only recently has our discipline left behind its tendency to look for homogenized cultural units. This has allowed anthropologists to focus more on the shades of grey of people's interaction and place. This is of critical significance in the development, and possibly survival, of our discipline, as it can become a vehicle to aid the increasingly complex transnational public sphere by facilitating such interconnections.

Anthropology's thick perspective on reality's polyphony is specially needed in our 'network society' (Castells [1996] 2000; Dijk [1991] 2006). The idea of global interconnectedness has spread throughout the academic world during these last decades (Giddens 1990). Just as in previous stages of Euro-American academic production there existed 'master metaphors' about life and society such as 'the machine', 'system', 'structure', 'market' or 'organism', today's metaphor seems to be the 'network'. Several academic disciplines have used it as a theoretical model to observe complex relations that currently abound. It has also shed a new light on the past, as historical events and social structures are being reconsidered through a focus on their network structures (McNeill and McNeill 2003). This positive appreciation of the network as a human feature has also reached the study of maps. In her study of the cartography of ancient empires, Smith (2005) argues that it was misleading to consider such polities as bounded within a specific territory as was marked in a map. She suggests that it is more relevant to study empires through a network structure, as their 'boundaries were flexible, porous, and constantly redefined' (Smith 2005: 833).

This context serves to point to anthropology's potential for mapping social relations. In the case of advocacy networks, such mapping entails a focus on 'solidarity'. Recent scholarly work on these issues has pointed towards the use of the gift theory to understand altruism and the will to help others (Komter 2005). What would follow, then, is an aim to understand such maps of relations. It is not a case of network analysis (Barnes [1968] 1969; Boissevain and Mitchell 1973), but rather of a study of network structures among activists and politically engaged individuals working within civil organizations or on a personal basis. As was mentioned above, these groupings are innovating the way professional political practice is carried out, while having a direct influence in communal life. The fact that the groups are fluid, that is in constant change and adaptation, makes them hard to pin down and study as solid units. That is why the idea of a map as a photograph, at a particular time and place, becomes relevant. Drawing on Foucault and Derrida, some cartographers have argued that the process of mapping is more about 'creating, rather than simply revealing, knowledge' (Kitchin and Dodge 2007: 332). It is therefore suggested here that by analysing advocacy networks, anthropologists can create maps that in turn provide guidelines for advocacy networks.

This potential contribution can help capture the social dynamics that allow for advocacy networks to come together and subsist. So far, this type of network has relied on the experience of its most skilled members. The life expectancy of these networks varies according to the clarity of its purpose for all those involved. If one has clear aims and projects and appeals to all its members and stakeholders, then most organizations that comprise it will remain together for a longer period. If its aims are vague and its projects do not take off, however, then it will slowly wane until it disappears (or only appears in papers as 'advocracy' – advocacy bureaucracy). Furthermore, a network may be so successful that its discourse and symbols overflow its own capacities and structures, thus leading to its dispersion. For all these processes, a key element is good intercultural communication, in order to avoid easy misunderstandings or mutual prejudices and distrust. There are other factors that influence their performance, but public anthropology is especially relevant to address the ones described above.

As new organizational forms, furthermore, their characteristics and functioning are still being created and experimented with.

This is where anthropological insights may result in maps that in turn provide a sense of direction that help their members recognize risks and advantages of certain decisions or paths. It entails an engagement of the sort Eriksen (2006: 130) claims as a potential contribution of our discipline: 'Anthropology can teach humility and empathy, and also the ability to listen, arguably one of the scarcest resources in the rich parts of the world these days'.

Some would say that life does not need a map. The logic behind maps is that every path taken is made easier when there is an idea of where it leads, or of other possible routes. Political philosophy, for example, started as a simple reflection on the way society co-existed. By classifying reality, it made it easier to think about what was possible, desirable or convenient for societies to improve their organization and governance. It thus became a normative arena by moving into what should or ought to be (Miller 2003). Many would say that it is impossible to think of anthropology as a normative discipline. Its descriptions and theorizations have more of an explanatory vein. The debate on the use of our discipline is usually more about its application to practical issues (van Willigen [1993] 2002) or its engagement with the public sphere (Eriksen 2006). In both issues, as in other discussions about the role and aims of the discipline, the concern of critics is mainly restricted to ideological stances and the uses of theories. Many anthropologists, however, aspire to a sort of dispassion in their descriptions (Geertz 1995). But, are descriptions not already types of abstract maps?

There is a strong humanistic heritage within our discipline. This sole fact provides it with a sort of normative stand. Its main moral stance follows Enlightenment values and a philosophical pursuit of the truth. Some argue that the grand scheme of anthropology is to prove the existence of 'Sameness' among all of humanity (Argyrou 2002), thus refuting racism and ethnocentrism. In an evolution of democratic ideals and practice, advocacy networks are reclaiming the public sphere for citizens of different backgrounds and places. Their efforts are about making bridges among those interested in and affected by specific issues. In doing so, they are themselves putting into practice the dialogue that they ask for. Their network structure allows for an ongoing crisscrossing of mutual influences, references and shared data and information, but also conflict and contestations. They are certainly moving into new terrain, by forcing governments and society at large to take them seriously, while avoiding becoming static institutions. By mapping their actions and interactions, we are not merely describing spaces and relations between their components but also helping to shape them.

References

Acosta, R. (2007), 'Managing Dissent: Advocacy Networks in the Brazilian Amazon and the Mediterranean' (PhD diss., University of Oxford).

Argyrou, V. (2002) *Anthropology and the Will to Meaning: A Postcolonial Critique*. London: Pluto Press.

Barnes, J. A. [1968] (1969), 'Networks and political process', in *Local-level politics: Social and cultural perspectives,* (ed.) M. J. Swartz (London: University of London Press).

Boissevain, J. and J. Clyde Mitchell (eds.) (1973), *Network Analysis Studies in Human Interaction* (The Hague: Mouton).

Borofsky, R. (2007), Public Anthropology (A Personal Account), in Public Anthropology <http://www.publicanthropology.com/Defining/publicanth-07Oct10.htm> (accessed 11 June 2009).

Castells, M. [1996] (2000), *The Information Age: Economy, Society and Culture. Volume I. The Rise of the Network Society* (Oxford and Malden: Blackwell Publishers).

Dijk, J. van [1991] (2006), *The Network Society: Social Aspects of New Media* (London: Sage).

Eriksen, T. H. (2006), *Engaging Anthropology: The Case for a Public Presence* (Oxford and New York: Berg).

Geertz, C. (1995), *After the Fact: Two Countries, Four Decades, One Anthropologist* (Cambridge, MA: Harvard University Press).

Giddens, A. (1990), *The Consequences of Modernity* (Cambridge: Polity Press).

IPAM (2006), 'Apresentação – Missão e o Instituto'. Instituto de Pesquisa Ambiental da Amazônia <http://www.ipam.org.br/ipam/missao.php> (accessed 16 May 2006).

ISA (2009), 'Quem somos'. Instituto Socioambiental <http://www.socioambiental.org> (accessed 11 June 2009).

Keck, M. and K. Sikkink (eds) (1998) *Activists beyond Borders: Advocacy Networks in International Politics*. Ithaca, NY/London: Cornell University Press.

Khagram, S., Riker, J. V. and Sikkink, K. (eds.) (2002), *Restructuring World Politics: Transnational Social Movements, Networks, and Norms* (Minneapolis and London: University of Minnesota Press).

Kitchin, R. and Dodge, M. (2007), 'Rethinking Maps', *Progress in Human Geography* 31, no. 3: 331–344.

Komter, A. (2005), *Social Solidarity and the Gift*. Cambridge: Cambridge University Press.

Lisansky, J. (1990), *Migrants to Amazonia: Spontaneous Colonization in the Brazilian Frontier* (Boulder, San Francisco and London: Westview Press).

McNeill, J. R. and McNeill, W. H. (2003), *The Human Web. A Bird's-eye View of World History* (New York and London: Norton).

Miller, D. (2003), *Political Philosophy: A Very Short Introduction* (Oxford: Oxford University Press).

Mosse, D. (2005), *Cultivating Development: An Ethnography of Aid Policy and Practice* (London and Ann Arbor: Pluto Press).

Riles, A. (2000), *The Network Inside Out* (Michigan: University of Michigan Press).

Schwartzman, S. and Zimmerman, B. (2005), 'Conservation Alliance with Indigenous Peoples in the Amazon', *Conservation Biology* 19, no. 3 (June): 721–727.

Smith, M. L. (2005), 'Networks, Territories, and the Cartography of Ancient States', *Annals of the Association of American Geographers* 95, no. 4: 832–849.

Tsing, A. L. (2005), *Friction: An Ethnography of Global Connection* (Princeton and Oxford: Princeton University Press).

van Willigen, J. [1993] (2002), *Applied Anthropology: An Introduction* (Westport, CT: Greenwood).

'Y Ikatu Xingu (2007), O que é <http://www.yikatuxingu.org.br/a-campanha> (accessed 11 June 2009).

Lessons from Vicos

Billie Jean Isbell

World Politics and the Cornell Peru Project

This article describes the Cornell Peru Project of 1952 and the subsequent return of Cornell to Vicos in 2005. After a survey and search for an appropriate community in 1949, Vicos in the department of Ancash in northern Peru was chosen in 1952 and Allan Holmberg, the chair of the Department of Anthropology at Cornell, signed a lease for the hacienda Vicos for US$600 a year. Subsequently the Cornell Peru Project became a model for integrated development involving cultural and biological anthropology, archaeology, agronomy, economics, political science, psychology and sociology. However, as this article discusses, integrated development has subsequently been heavily criticised. Cornell had a presence in Vicos until 1966 and Doughty (2002) calculates that the project cost an estimated US$711,000 or US$35 per capita per year and it is not clear whether this figure includes the extensive funding for independent researchers over the almost 15 years of the project. As Alan Holmberg stated:

> In 1952, as part of a research program in Cultural Applied Science, Cornell University, in collaboration with the Indigenous Institute of Peru, arranged to rent Vicos, a publicly owned hacienda on which previous observational studies had been made, for an initial period of five years. Broadly speaking, the purpose of embarking on this experience was twofold: on the theoretical side, it was hoped to conduct some form of experimental research on the processes of modernization now on the

march in so many parts of the world; on the practical side, it was hoped to assist the community to shift for itself from a position of relative dependence and submission in a highly restricted and provincial world to a position of relative independence and freedom within the larger framework of Peruvian national life. ([1964] 1971: 21)

Vicos was part of a larger 'Cultural Applied Science' effort at Cornell that grew out of Cornell's long history of agricultural missionaries who introduced crops and technologies in China between 1928 and 1937 (Thompson 1969: 150). The larger comparative project on development and integration took place in five cultural regions and was initially directed by Morris Opler who had come to Cornell after serving three years in the War Information Office (1943–1946). The comparative project was carried out with Lauriston Sharp and Alexander Leighton, who also had experience in the War Information Office and the War Relocation Office that managed the internment camps for Japanese Americans (see Davies 2001 and Ross 2005, 2008 for fuller historical accounts). The regions chosen were: Bang Chan, Thailand; Senapur, India; Nova Scotia, Canada; the Navaho of the American Southwest; and Vicos near Huaraz, Peru (Avila 2002: 419).[1] The project coincided with the beginning of the Cold War with the underlying ideology and fears generated by the war against communism that these underdeveloped regions would be susceptible to communism (Ross 2005). The rise of communism in China, the Cuban Revolution, Arbez's modest land reform in Guatemala in 1952 (that the CIA derailed), and the Bolivian revolution (also in 1952) were worrisome. But even with these events, modernization theory was guided by the erroneous belief that peasants could not be their own agents of change due to their conservative values. Furthermore, it was believed that the transfer of technologies to improve production, coupled with controlling population growth, would be sufficient to deflect the communist threat and the growing unrest over distribution of land and resources.

When Cornell arrived in 1949 to conduct the initial survey, the hacienda was an unprofitable enterprise. The patrones were absentee landlords with little concern for the education and wellbeing of their peasants. Even though the plan was for Alan Holmberg and the team of researchers to be present for five years, during which time Vicos would purchase the hacienda, in spite of continuous negotiations on the part of the Cornell team, the hacienda purchase took 10 years to realize. One of the events that took place in 1961 was that Edward Kennedy intervened with the president of Peru. Kennedy was not the only prominent North American to arrive in Vicos. More than 500 foreigners arrived in Vicos during the Cornell Peru Project to visit the 'miracle of modernization'. For example, in 1963, Charles Kuralt of CBS travelled to Vicos to make a film called 'So that Men are Free' for Walter Cronkite's 'You Are There' series <http://courses.cit.cornell.edu/vicosperu/vicos-site/cornellperu_page_1.htm>.

Seventeen hundred peasants who were close to starvation were listed in the lease as chattel. Today the population is approximately 5,500 and no one is starving but health and nutritional levels are not high. In 1952, even though the proceeds from the hacienda were supposed to support a hospital in Huaraz, the capital of the region, the earnings on the enterprise were in fact shared by the group of managers for whom the Indian population was required to serve as household servants or as field hands. Also, the *patrones* could sell the labour of the resident serfs to mines, textile factories or other businesses. For example, Vicosinos were required to work in the textile mills that produced linen for the Second World War. The Quechua-speaking Indians living on the land were serfs to the managers, or *patrones*, of the so-called publicly owned hacienda. The boundaries of the hacienda were guarded so that the serfs could not escape.

Assumptions of the Project

Barbara Lynch (1982: 21–22), in her excellent assessment of the project, states that in an *ex post facto* analytical framework Holmberg, Vázquez and Dobyns [1964] (1971) set up two polar ideal types defined as medieval and Western Civilization with a continuum between the two. Vicos was seen as an isolated 'anachronism in the modern world' (Holmberg [1964] 1971: 32), not as product of modern power relations. The view was commonly held by social scientists of the time. In actuality Vicos was integrated into the national society. Also, Lynch cites Mangin's (1955) and Himes' (1972) assessments that Vicosinos were better off economically than many other hacienda *peones* and communities in the highlands. They had access to more agricultural and pasture land as well as abundant water. Like other Andean populations, Vicos was integrated into the Peruvian economy as a source of labour for regional public works projects, for the mines of Conchucos, for commercially oriented haciendas on the western slopes of the Andes and for the Santa Corporation linen factory at Pati. The terms of this integration were generally unfavourable, but far less so than for many other Indian populations (Lynch 1982: 22).

By the time Cornell left in 1966, the project team believed the goal to guide the 1,700 Indian serfs living on the hacienda Vicos into the twentieth century had been achieved. We now see that the assumption that Vicos was an anachronism from the past was wrong. Moreover, they had been political actors since the turn of the century and had made numerous appeals to the Peruvian state. The earliest evidence we have is a photograph dating around 1913 showing a delegation petitioning the President of Peru for their ancestral land. And as stated above the population was integrated into the labour force but the anticipated industrial development in the region that Holmberg expected to absorb the excess population in Vicos from population growth and commercialization of agriculture did not take place (Martinez 1989). A major contribution of the project was that it made the conditions of subjugation of the hacienda system visible to a larger public. Doughty (2002, fn.3) points out that at the time of the project the hacienda system survived in some form in Colombia, Venezuela, Ecuador, Peru, Chile, Paraguay, Argentina, Uruguay and Brazil. The system was abolished in Bolivia in the 1952 revolution and the Cuban revolution of 1959 was right around the corner.

Since one of Cornell's stated goals in Vicos was to study modernization, the hacienda labour structure was kept intact for one year without the obligation of forced labour but Cornell retained the hacienda overseer, Enrique Luna, who was appointed manager of production for the commercialization of potatoes to be sold in the Lima market. A photograph of him with a raised whip in hand was published in the Cornell Alumni News in May 1962 with the caption: 'Before They Took Orders from a *Mestizo* Foreman' (Figure 1). According to Doughty (2002) and Mangin (2006), Luna changed his behaviour and attitude towards Vicosinos as the Cornell project progressed. But according to participants in the Living Memory Project directed by Florencia Zapata (Zapata 2005), Luna is still hated today for his harsh treatment of Vicosinos 50 years ago. One of the few historical monuments in Vicos is the pillory, where Vicosinos were publicly whipped by Luna.

This discrepancy in historical perspectives was debated during a conference held at Cornell University in 2006 entitled: 'Sustainability: Lessons from Vicos'. The conference was attended by Vicosinos and three generations of researchers who had worked in the community of Vicos.[2] Keeping Luna as overseer raises the issue of the ethics of research methodologies. Alan Holmberg and his team opted for the priority of science, rationalizing that keeping Luna would facilitate their comparative methodology to study the hacienda production system before and after they introduced 'modern' agricultural methods to the community. Vicosinos were not consulted about keeping Luna as overseer, possibly because none of the initial North American researchers who began the project in Vicos learned Quechua. However, Mario Vásquez, a young native speaker of Quechua from the region, joined the project and began his studies as Holmberg's graduate student at Cornell. He is remembered by Vicosinos with respect and fondness. For example, during the 2006 conference at Cornell in response to how Enrique Luna is represented in the Living Memory book, Doughty recounted how in 1957 when funding from the Carnegie Foundation ended there were no funds to pay the rent on the hacienda, Vázquez and Luna paid the rent out of their own pockets. Doughty felt that Luna had changed. Vicosinos however remembered the various beneficial actions of Vázquez but not those of Luna.

William Stein, who joined the project later, is the only North American researcher who learned Quechua. I think it is significant that he has published a critical volume on the Cornell Peru Project

Figure 1: Luna Giving Work Orders

(Stein 2000, 2003) in which he concludes that, although the project did produce better living conditions for Vicos in the form of a school, medical clinic and housing for teachers, integration into the local region declined. He argued that possibly the project also prolonged the life of some Vicosinos and improved the quality of life of many. On the other hand, Vicos has grown and changed and was not much different from thousands of other Andean communities; they exported their population to urban centres: they fought to improve their lives in a poor country that is burdened with an enormous foreign debt and did not have the resources to provide services to villagers (2000: 395).

The number of Peruvian and North America researchers between 1951 and 1966 numbered 89 according to Paul Doughty (2002) and ministerial staff numbered 16.[3] The Project personnel worked with mostly young men, largely excluding monolingual Quechua-speaking women and the very poor, especially from the agricultural innovations introduced by Cornell to facilitate potato commercialization. They did introduce a Singer sewing machine and teach women to sew. Doughty states that the original project was participatory; however, decisions about the direction of the project were made by researchers not by Vicosinos.

The Most Significant Achievement of the Project: Improvements in Education

It is my opinion that improving education has been the most significant and lasting achievement of the project. Today over 30 Vicosinos are studying in post-secondary institutions, and most of those who receive higher education return to Vicos. The Cornell team set out to improve education by building a school to accommodate 250 students using communal labour, to replace the old school which fewer than 30 boys attended (see Vásquez 1965). One of the primary goals of the Cornell Peru Project (CPP) was to integrate the Indian population into the national culture. But, Cornell could not predict the continued racism that has led to the rejection of the indigenous population, their heritage and cultural practices. Even with an education, Vicosinos find it difficult to integrate into the national culture at the level commensurate with their education. Several post secondary students are seeking further education in tourism that will provide employment that values their heritage, allows them to maintain their ties to Vicos, and to integrate into national culture as well. About thirty Vicosinos live in Alexandria, Virginia. The wave of migration to the U.S. began when one of the first young men to complete high school married one of the women on the Cornell team. He later completed Howard University and has a business in the area. His sister owns a restaurant called Huarascarán in Alexandria. They return to Vicos for vacations and have built a three-story house in 'downtown' Vicos (Doughty, personal communication). I heard expressions of resentment that such an ostentatious house was built by Vicosinos who have left the community.

Photographs often provide clues of the underlying assumptions of a development programme. Schoolboys in their uniforms stand beneath the Cornell University Seal that was proudly displayed in the new school (Figure 2). What does this photograph signify? Certainly Cornell's presence, but perhaps it signifies Cornell and education as the pinnacle of modernization.

Another staged photograph (Figure 3) depicts the progression from traditional, poor, ragged and illiterate Indian status to modern, educated, integrated into national, *mestizo* society, showing three boys on three steps with the one on the lowest step dressed in rags

Figure 2: School Boys with Cornell Seal

Figure 3: From Serf to Modernity

and looking dejected. The boy on the highest step is dressed in a full school uniform (modelled after military uniforms) with the boy on the middle step 'in-between' – he has on a traditional vest and woven belt, but proudly wears the school uniform, complete with hat. Both boys wear the homemade leather thong sandals, while the poorest boy on the bottom is bare foot. Shoes were the most expensive marker of modernity.

Other CPP photographs explicitly compare levels of modernization as in the following (Figure 4) taken in 1963 of two young brothers: the one dressed in 'western clothes' is the most educated young man in Vicos who is also a veteran of the Peruvian Army. His brother wears the traditional clothing. The older brother insists that his younger brother get an education and join the military reserves. The military was promoted by the Cornell Project staff as

Figure 4: Brothers Dressed in Traditional and Modern Clothing

a means of integrating Vicosino men into the national culture and economy; staff believed that once men served in the military they would become part of the urban work force.

Health and Nutrition

Health issues were a major item on the Cornell team's agenda. A new health clinic, with a visiting doctor, nurse and dentist and a school lunch programme were established. In Dobyns and Vázquez (1963) immediate improvements in nutrition were claimed. The Cornell team contrasted the arrival of modern medicine with such traditional practices as shown in Figure 5 – a woman curer rubbing a patient's body with a guinea pig. She then cuts open the

Figure 5: Woman Curer Rubbing Guinea Pig on Patient's Body

guinea pig to diagnose the disease. It was believed that the guinea pig absorbs the patient's disease into its organs. A doctor is shown giving the same patient an inoculation – Figure 6. These photographs were published in the *Cornell University Alumni News* in 1962 to contrast modern and traditional medicine.

What the Cornell team was not aware of was the vast Vicosino knowledge of medicinal plants that they grew and collected. Today we know that Peru is recognized as one of the twelve most biodiverse regions of the world. Over 4000 species of native plants are known, providing low-cost medicine to 80 percent of Peru's population. In Dobyns and Vázquez (1963) numerous scientific research projects linked to the Cornell Project were enumerated, involving the Vicos population. The studies that resulted in intervention included: parasitological testing showing that infection was universal as well as nutritional studies measuring the levels of malnutrition. Clinics were established to treat these conditions. However, numerous other studies were carried out for scientific purposes: blood, human growth and development, and even a

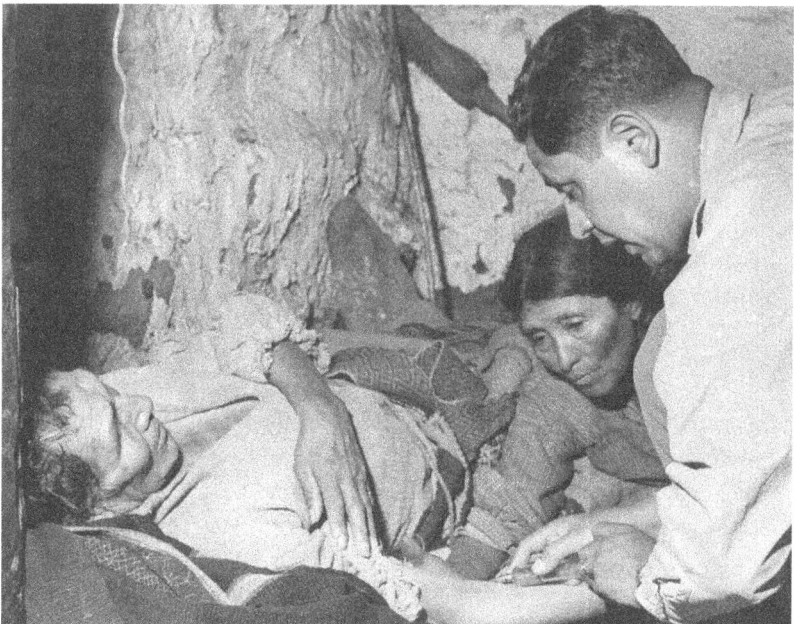

Figure 6: A Doctor Giving a Shot to the Same Patient

personality study conducted by the Sullivan Psychoanalytical Institute of New York City in 1960. Alarmingly, during the Vicos conference in 2006 Mangin mentioned that Park Davis pharmaceutical company tested a drug to treat parasites in Vicos. According to Mangin (2006) this practice was common during the 1950s and 1960s.

In his publication of 2002, Doughty stated that nutrition levels were currently high and pointed out that a small government hospital was accessible to all Vicosinos. However, recent nutritional and health surveys in Vicos indicate that malnutrition and intestinal parasites remain high among children (Zapata, personal communication). This is most likely due to lack of sanitation, plumbing and clean water. Even though the community has initiated a water purification programme in response to mining pollution, parasites continue to be a problem indicating that they are not addressing parasites in the drinking water.

Democracy and Self Determination

In the introduction to *Peasants, Power, and Applied Social Change: Vicos as a Model,* Dobyns, Doughty, and Lasswell stated:

> The role of power in opening the door to change was appreciated by Cornell Peru Project leadership right from the beginning when it assumed the position of patron of the Vicos manor with all the absolute privileges that the role contained. Through the planned devolution of that power to the people of Vicos, Project leadership was able to modify other areas of life which had been very rigidly controlled. Thus, power is the key factor whether one speaks of peaceful or of violent change. Writing in a comparative study of peasant revolution of this century, Eric Wolf says: 'The poor peasant or the landless laborer who depends on a landlord for the largest part of his livelihood, or the totality of it, has no tactical power: he is completely within the power domain of his employer, without sufficient resources of his own to serve him as resources in the power of struggle. Poor peasants and landless laborers, therefore, are unlikely to pursue the course of rebellion *unless* they are able to rely on some external power to challenge the power which constrains them.' (1969:

20). The Cornell Peru Project provided that important external source of power constituting a social umbrella under which the people of Vicos were able to alter their lives to their greater satisfaction, and without the imminent threat of tragedy and retribution to discourage them as it had before. ([1964] 1971: 15–16)

The above quote clearly states the view Holmberg and the project staff held regarding the importance of power relations. They expected 'planned devolution of power' that would transform their position as patrons of the hacienda and allow Vicosinos to develop self-determination, which they have. Moreover, Vicosinos have the reputation in the region as being politically aggressive outside of Vicos, holding several regional offices and working to have Vicos become an independent district. But we must ask whether Non-governmental organizations are providing the 'external source of power' today that Wolf thought was necessary for rebellion and the Cornell personnel thought provided an umbrella under which the community could change their lives. The 1952 quote above by Holmberg demonstrates the he saw Vicosinos moving from a subjugated position to one of relative independence and freedom. However, barriers to integration into the national culture remain and as stated earlier, most Vicosinos who receive post secondary education return to Vicos. The governance structure representing the 10 barrios or sectors of the hacienda of Vicos that was set up with an elected village council exists today. However, the *consejo* or council changes frequently because of internal disputes or accusations of corruption, making it difficult to ensure continuity of decisions and programmes. Mechanisms for accountability are not in place.

Nevertheless, Vicos has taken successful collective action against powerful mining companies. While we were in Vicos in February of 2008, we learned that the Toma La Mano mining company was about to pay Vicos the last of three compensation payments totalling one million dollars. The community voted that the funds were to be dispersed in three payments to all households. At the time of our visit, none of the funds were allocated for public works even though several needs have been discussed in public meetings, including the need for Internet access. The level of political participation and community organizational skills is a long way from the conditions that the Cornell Peru Project personnel found when Cornell took control of the hacienda in 1952.

Agricultural Innovations

The story of Cornell's agricultural innovations is complex and provides us with a cautionary tale. The CPP in Vicos is paradigmatic of the Green Revolution because if you take less than a 10-year view the increase in production was a success. But the intensive technologies were not sustainable over time. The commercialization of potato production for the Lima market with mono-cropping, the introduction of Cornell 'improved' varieties, chemical fertilizers and insecticides was an initial success. In 1954, the first year of these new techniques, production doubled. Ten years later, Vicos was providing two percent of the total potatoes sold in the Lima market but production began to fall shortly thereafter in the mid-1960s and eventually failed due to insect infestations to which the introduced varieties were not resistant. Nevertheless, the 10 years of commercialization of production allowed Vicos to purchase the hacienda in 1962 after seven years of difficult negotiations with the Benefit Society, which at one point raised the price 900 percent. From a capitalist short-term perspective, the rise in production was an enormous success. But, if you take a longer view, it was ultimately a failure. The introduction of chemicals and mono-cropping almost destroyed the biodiversity of the region and caused damage to the fragile environment. Vicosinos are engaged in projects to preserve their biodiversity and redress the damage to their environment. Their projects were described during the Vicos conference in 2006. An example is the project on biodiversity and culture in the Callejón de Huaylas initiated by the NGO Asociación Urpichallay (1999).

Women and Biodiversity

Vicosina women and the very poor (the 100 families without access to plots) were excluded from the project to commercialize potatoes in favour of working with male heads of households. Florence Babb ([1985] 1999) and Barbara Lynch (1982) both pointed to the methodological failings of such exclusions in their publications. However, the exclusion of women and the very poor became an unforeseen benefit. They continued their ancient practices of seed conservation that eventually saved the 120 varieties of potatoes and numerous other crops that they produced.

Today we know that the Vicosina women not only manage household economies but also have great knowledge about the plant world. They are ultimately responsible for seed selection and preservation. Every year fairs to exchange seeds are held and people travel from across the country to participate. Variability is celebrated and shared through these exchanges. Unlike the capitalist notion of ownership protected by patents, new varieties are exchanged. Archaeological evidence suggests that Quechua-speaking farmers understood from ancient times that maintaining biodiversity in their seed collections was critical to survival – and were willing to travel hundreds of miles to guarantee it. Agents of change in the 1950s and 1960s, on the other hand, thought they could trump nature by using chemical additives.

Unintended Consequences of the Cornell Peru Project

The Cornell Project began their modernization efforts in 1952 and remained in Vicos until 1966 without anticipating the agrarian reform of 1969 that expropriated neighbouring haciendas and al-located the land to the serfs that lived on them. Most Vicosinos believed that they were still paying off the enormous long-term debt while their neighbours received land free. However, during the Living Memory Project, Vicosinos learned that the debt had been discharged by the Peruvian Government.

Today we are aware that the hope that 'modern' high-intensity agriculture with chemical inputs and mono-cropping would solve the hunger problem in the so-called underdeveloped regions of the world has not been realized. Of course we are becoming rapidly aware of the costs to the environment and to human health from the use of chemical fertilizers, herbicides and pesticides required in high-intensity agriculture. According to David Tilman (1998: 211–212)[4] of the University of Minnesota, it is unclear whether high-intensity agriculture can be sustained because of the loss of soil fertility, the erosion of soil, the increased incidence of crop and livestock diseases and the serious effects of nitrogen on terrestrial, freshwater and marine ecosystems, because half to two-thirds of the nitrogen applied to fields enters these ecosystems. Moreover, Tilman and his colleagues estimate that it would take 200 years of natural succession whereby fields are left abandoned and invaded by successive populations of native vegetation for fields to recover pre-agricultural carbon and nitrogen levels. Vicosinos have experienced these unfortunate consequences of Cornell's introduction of chemicals. It appears that these chemicals in combination with nitrogen commonly found in groundwater may have a broad range of effects on the immune, endocrine and nervous systems.[5]

The failure of the Cornell's potato project to be sustainable over time was an important factor in precipitating rejection of outside interventions. However, according to the interviews conducted for the Living Memory Project, Vicosinos declared that the misunderstood actions of one Peace Corps volunteer who borrowed funds from his father to renovate the hot baths and hotel at Chancos led to their expulsion in 1964 before Cornell left in 1966.[6] They believed that the volunteer was attempting to take possession of the property. They also declared that in 1973 corrupt state administrators of a cattle project stole funds from the community and that was probably the final link in the chain that barred outsiders. Vicosinos finally said: 'Ya Basta!' Enough! They closed their doors to all outside intervention.

Cornell's Return to Vicos

In 2005 after five years of discussions with the community of Vicos, I initiated a project to return to Vicos to document the history of the Cornell Peru Project in collaboration with The Mountain Institute and with Florencia Zapata who developed the Living Memory Project during her two-year tenure at Cornell as a visiting fellow. We collaboratively developed several motivating questions for Cornell's return to Vicos: what were the successes and failures of the Cornell Peru Project? What have been the lasting impacts and how are people of Vicos faring today? What do contemporary efforts of development look like? Can the history of that project teach us anything as the world struggles to address poverty, health and development issues? The Cornell Peru Project in Vicos is one of the best-documented case studies of directed change and it can provide the bases for beginning a discussion of what issues have remained and what has changed.

Participating in those discussions were Vicosino leaders, The Mountain Institute (TMI), and Urpichallay, a Peruvian NGO that has worked in the region for 15 years. The participatory methodologies that we adopted contrasted markedly to that of the CPP. Our discussions centred on the priorities of the community within the framework of what Cornell University could offer as a participating partner. Two initiatives were collectively agreed upon: (1) building a Vicos website that would document not only the history of the Cornell Project but also describe the contemporary development projects chosen by Vicosinos, and (2) developing the participatory Living Memory Project that would allow Vicos to explore their own history (see Zapata 2005).

A website was created that addresses the history of directed change in Vicos initiated by Cornell University as well as videos and interviews of current development projects chosen by the community http://courses.cit.cornell.edu/vicosperu/vicos-site/ (Isbell and Zapata 2005). Also included in the site are the full texts in Spanish of the oral histories recorded in Spanish and Quechua of community members, which have been recorded and printed as a book that the participants designed. Copies of the book, *Memorias de la Comunidad de Vicos,* were then provided to every household in Vicos as well as to the schools. The volume is also available online in English translation on the web site above. Therefore, fifty years of history is available online from the Vicosinos' diverse points of view that provide an interesting comparison with the vast quantity of research material written by academics, much of which is housed in the Kroch Rare Manuscript Library of Cornell University. A spin-off of Zapata's Living Memory Project has been the return of digitized research and photos to Vicos. The community built a local museum called Casa de los Abuelos which houses these materials, but it is only opened when visiting tourists arrive. Evidently, it is viewed as something that interests outsiders and not locals. Hopefully, it will be used in the future by the schools.

An ongoing project initiated in 2006 and directed by Florencia Zapata of TMI with Cornell participation and support involves a committee of Vicosinos who are working to locate and digitize historical records to validate their land claims and establish legal boundaries. One of the major motivations for the creation of the digital archive is that Vicosinos want Vicos to constitute an independent *distrito* (a Peruvian governmental unit similar to a county). They also understand the importance of legally documenting their land as privatization of land threatens the future of peasant communities who make up 37 percent of the population and hold 39.8 percent of agricultural lands in the highlands. With increased population and with the government's push to privatize communal lands in 1996, Vicos is experiencing an acute shortage of available agricultural land. To gain usufruct of land one must be a *comunero* and participate in the communal structure of the community by attending meetings, work parties and holding office. That causes a dilemma for those with enough education to work outside of Vicos who want to maintain their membership in the community. If they work too far away to stay active in the communal structure, they lose their membership and also lose access to land.

In response to Vicosinos' expression of urgency over the need to provide historical documentation of their communal status, I applied for and received a second Innovation Grant from Cornell in 2008 to continue collaborative work with TMI, Urpillachay and Vicos to organize workshops to digitize historical documents and facilitate the creation of a digital archive with the participation of Danielle Mericle, the production manager for Olin Library's Digital Media Group. She directed workshops not only in Vicos and Marcará at Urpillachay but also in Lima at the Archivo Nacional. We hope to create an open access portal in the library system allowing Vicosinos, researchers and students to deposit, access and communicate digitally. The workshops in Peru were the first step in the process to build such global communication. In Vicos, 35 participants attended including six women and 29 males ranging in age from 11 to 67 years old. Sixteen of the participants had used a computer before and eight had experience on the Internet. The core group has been working with Zapata in national and regional archives to copy documents relevant to the community. They developed and broadcasted a radio programme in Quechua about their efforts. The workshop took place in the new computer centre built with communal labour with funding from a Cuadalos Mining Company that purchased 15 computers as part of a compensation package after winning a lawsuit. When we arrived, the computer centre was locked and the instructor was not being paid by the Toma La Mano Mining Company as agreed upon because Vicos was engaged in a dispute with the owner and had burned him in effigy in the plaza.

Final Reflections

CPP's original plan was to be involved in Vicos for five years but they remained for 15 years with legions of researchers pursuing individual goals, leaving little behind of their research (Mangin [1979] 1988). For example, archaeological research that was conducted in the region certainly mapped areas that would have been useful to the local communities but these researches were not shared with Vicosinos. During the Vicos conference the representatives from Vicos conducted a search of Vicos Archive and we have digitized documents for the digital archive they have established in the community. Communities in the region will no longer tolerate researchers without coming to an agreement on the benefits that will be delivered to them. That lesson from Vicos and other communities like it has been learned well. Perhaps one of the most interesting lessons learned has been to uncover the different versions of the histories of the Vicos Project: The community constructed a history of the project from their collective memories that differed significantly from the history held by the researchers involved. Comparing such histories could guide contemporary development (for example, see the forthcoming volume, *Haciendo Anthropología Trabajar: La Experiencía Andina*, T. Greaves and R. Bolton, editors, Lima, IEP).

An academic institution like Cornell, unlike an NGO, a state or international agency lacks the experience and skills to work with local populations for long-term development. Nor can academics maintain their presence in the field continuously for sustainability – an issue in Vicos. However, universities have the capacities to act as mediators between local institutions and local populations. We can participate in providing basic research, historical and comparative perspectives that local institutions and populations may not be able to achieve alone. The history of the CPP, like many histories, teaches us that what may look like success in the short term (10 years) may not be sustainable in the long run. Sound record-keeping is essential to establish an historical basis for continual evaluation. Universities must share those records with local populations. The CPP attempted to return research to Vicos but the community was not ready at that point in time to receive the data. Now they realize the value of historical records. Collaborating with TMI to work towards establishing a digital archive and to provide advice on digitizing was our goal during the 2008 visit to Vicos. Cornell will continue to return the records to Vicos that the community prioritize.

University faculty staff and graduate students often have difficulty working within an open learning paradigm. Within academia it is a question of ownership of research, theses and innovations. In Vicos and in many other parts of the world, that kind of individual ownership is not recognized. Knowledge is collectively owned and shared. This perhaps is one of the largest obstacles to collaborative research and application. During my 15 years of working with Cornell's International Institute of Food, Agriculture and Development (CIIFAD), whose aim was to form interdisciplinary teams to work in Latin American, Africa and Asia to support research and development efforts, I discovered that academics often found it difficult to step outside of their disciplinary training and learn 'from the natives' – and the harder the science the more difficulty faculty had. But time and again we learned that 'the natives' had a lot to teach us and that the best innovations came from collaboration between users and sources of research, like universities.[7] The experiences of interdisciplinary work have led to greater participatory action research and a greater openness by academic disciplines involved to accept natives as collaborators.

Most Vicosinos are positive about the future and many have plans for micro enterprises. For their incipient ecotourism they need to be able to connect with tourists directly to avoid the control outsiders have exerted over Taquile (Zorn 2004). They hope that the move to embrace computer technology can accomplish that. One of the high-potential micro enterprises developing rapidly is organic production. An association of organic growers has been formed and, Beatriz Rojas, the former director of Urpillachay, informs me that young people from the region are receiving fellowships and training in Lima in organic production and marketing, restaurant management and cooking through the efforts of Gaston Ocurio, one of Peru's most successful chefs.

Finally, we do not know what events will flow from the introduction of the digital technology that we have facilitated in Vicos. We cannot assume universal access and differences in class structure could be exacerbated. In the spring of 2010, I will return to Peru as a Senior Specialist through the Fulbright Programme to facilitate workshops open to leaders from the Andean region on digitizing technologies and archival research that Vicosinos will participate in as teachers. Communities realize that they must provide historical documentation to validate their communal land claims in the face of privatization being pushed by Garcia's neoliberal government.

In conclusion, one of the long-term effects of the CCP is that Vicos learned to negotiate with outside agencies and articulate their demands clearly. Moreover, the expulsion of Cornell and other agents of change reinforced their own sense of empowerment. The successful lawsuit against Toma La Mano mining is evidence of that empowerment. However, the communal structure of Vicos has ironically resulted in the funds from that lawsuit being distributed among communal members and not being used for public benefit. Stable local governance and accountability continues to be a problem. Vicos leadership in the region speaks to their increase in education which is perhaps the most important lasting effect of the project but gains in health have not been as strong. Vicosinos consider themselves international citizens with connection in various parts of the world and perhaps Cornell's presence accelerated that process.

Notes

1. Avila's article is an excellent source for placing the Vicos project within the historical context of the development of Peruvian anthropology. For a full description of the research conducted in Vicos see Dobyns and Vázquez 1963. Doughty (2002) states that over 200 books and articles have been written about Vicos; however, it is significant that in 2005 and 2008, we found no evidence of that research existing in the community. Evidently, a filing cabinet of research was left in Vicos, but at some time the papers were dumped on the floor of the Holmberg-abandoned house in order for the filing cabinet to be used by the village council. Consult the video entitled 'The Holmberg House' on the Vicos website to see scenes that look like the archaeology of development. I have appended on the site a timeline of the project provided by Doughty. <http://courses.cit.cornell.edu/vicosperu/vicos-site/cornellperu_page_1.htm>.
2. For an early evaluation of the Vicos project see Lynch (1982).
3. I wish to thank Paul Doughty (1985 ms.) for providing this information. It is unclear how many of the Peruvian researchers and ministerial personnel were Quechua speakers.
4. <http://www.nature.com/nature/journal/v396/n6708/full/396211a0.html>
5. According to Kaplan and Morris in a U.S. News and World Report article published in 2000 (47–53) the increased prevalence of these neurotoxins in U.S. water is linked with increases in neurological disorders in American children. The authors link the toxins with the statistic, for example, that in California, reported cases of autism rose 210% between 1987 and 1998. The authors also note that in New York State, the number of children with learning disabilities rose 55 percent between 1983 and 1996. Statistics like these make researchers at The Mountain Institute wonder what might be happening to children exposed to neurotoxins in places like Vicos (personal communication). Did Cornell, following the paradigm of the Green Revolution, export potential health and environmental problems that outweigh the increased agricultural production that was achieved?

6. It is notable that the Peace Corps is currently posted in Vicos. In 2005 and 2006, Vicosinos complained about the laziness and lack of communal spirit of the volunteer. They said he lived off of them but did not work at all.

7. CIIFAD annual reports can be accessed at <http://ciifad.cornell.edu/about/annualreports/2004-2005/04-05_CIIFADar.pdf>

References

Asociación Urpichallay (1999), *Así Converso con mi chacra y mis semillas: la agrobiodiversidad en la Cuenca de Marcará: una perspectiva campesina* (Marcará: Urpichallay).

Avila, J. (2002), 'Los dilemmas del desarrollo: Antropología y promoción en el Perú', in *No Hay Pais Más Diverso: Compendio de Antropología Peruana,* (ed.) C. I. Degregori, Serie Perú Problema 27: 413–442 (Lima: IEP).

Babb, F. [1985] (1999), 'Mujeres y hombres en Vicos, Perú: Un caso de desarrollo desigual', *Género y Desarrollo II* (Lima: Pontifíca Universidad Católica del Perú).

Davies, W. (2001), 'Cornell's Field Seminar in Applied Anthropology: Social Scientists and American Indians in the Postwar Southwest', *Journal of the Southwest* 43, no. 3: 381–341.

Dobyns, H., Doughty, P. and Laswell, H. (eds.) [1964] (1971), *Peasants, Power, and Applied Social Change: Vicos as a Model* (Beverly Hills and London: Sage Publications).

Dobyns, H. and Vázquez, M. (1963), *'El Proyecto Perú – Cornell: personal y bibliografia, Cornell Peru Project* Pamphlet, no. 2, Ithaca, New York (Department of Anthropology, Cornell University).

Doughty, P. (2002), 'Ending Serfdom in Peru: The Struggle for Land and Freedom in Vicos', in *Contemporary Cultures and Societies of Latin America: A Reader in Social Anthropology of Middle and South America,* (ed.) D. Heath (Prospect Heights, Illinois: Waveland Press) 222–243.

Greaves, T. and Bolton, R. (eds.) (in press), *Haciendo Anthropología Trabajar: La Experiencia Andina* (Lima, IEP).

Himes, J. R. (1972), 'The Utilization of Research for Development: Two Case Studies in Rural Modernization and Agriculture in Peru' (PhD diss., Princeton University).

Holmberg, A. R. (1952), 'Proyecto Perú-Cornell en las ciencias sociales aplicadad', *Perú Indígena,* Nos. 5–6.

———— [1964] (1971),'Experimental Intervention in the Field', in *Peasants, Power, and Applied Social Change: Vicos as a Model,* (eds.) H. Dobyns, P. Doughty and H. Lasswell (Beverly Hills and London: Sage Publications).

Holmberg, A. R. (ed.) (1966), *Vicos: Metodo y Practica de Antropología Aplicada* (Lima, Peru: Estudios Andinos).

Isbell, B. J. and F. Zapata (2005), 'Vicos: A Virtual Tour from 1952 to the Present', website <http://courses.cit.cornell.edu/vicosperu/vicos-site>.

Kaplan, S. and Morris, J. (2000), 'Kids at Risk: Chemicals in the Environment Come under Scrutiny as the Number of Childhood Learning Problems Soars', U.S. and World Report 128, no. 24 (June 19): 47–53.

Lynch, B. (1982), *The Vicos Experiment: A Study of the Impacts of the Cornell–Peru Project in a Highland Community* (Washington, DC: AID Evaluation Special Study No. 7).

Mangin, W. (1955), 'Estratificación social en el Callejón de Huaylas', *Revista del Museo Nacional* 34: 174–189.

———— [1979] (1988), 'Thoughts on Twenty-four Years of Work in Peru: The Vicos Project and Me', in *It's All Relative: Readings in Social Anthropology* (Dubuque, IA: Kendall/Hunt Publishing).

———— (2006), Comments during conference discussion, 'Sustainability: Lessons from Vicos' (Ithaca: Cornell University).

Martinez, H. (1989), 'Vicos: continuidad y cambio', *Socialismo y Participación* 44: 149–160. (Lima: CEDEP)

Ross, E. B. (2005), 'Vicos as Cold War Strategy: Anthropology, Peasants and "Community Development"', *Anthropology in Action* 12, no. 3: 21–32

———— (2008), 'Peasants on Our Minds: Anthropology, the Cold War and the Myth of Conservatism', in *Anthropology at the Dawn of the Cold War: The Influence of Foundations, McCarthyism and the CIA,* (ed.) D. M. Wax (London and Ann Arbor: Pluto Press).

Stein, W. W. (2000), *Vicisitudes del Discurso del Desarrollo en el Perú: Una etnografía sobre la modernidad del Proyecto Vicos* (Lima: Sur Casa de Estudios del Socialismo).

———— (2003), *Deconstructing Development Discourse in Peru: A Meta-ethnography of the Modernity Project at Vicos* (Landman, MD: University Press of America).

Thompson, J. (1969), *While China Faced West, American Reformers in Nationalist China, 1928–1937* (Cambridge, MA: Harvard University Press).

Tillman, D. (1998), 'The Greening of the Green Revolution', *Nature* 396: 211–212.

Vásquez, M. (1965), *Educación Rural en el Callejón de Huaylas: Vicos* (Lima: Editorial Estudios Andinos).

—— (1971), 'The Interplay between Power and Wealth', in *Peasants, Power, and Applied Social Change: Vicos as a Model,* (eds.) H. Dobyns, P. Doughty and H. Lasswell (Beverly Hills and London: Sage Publications).

Wolf, E. R. (1969), *Peasant Wars of Twentieth Century* (New York: Harper and Row).

Zapata, F. with the community of Vicos (2005), *Memorias de la Comunidad de Vicos: Asi Recordamos con Alegría* (TMI, Urpichallay, Cornell University: Huaraz, Peru: Urpichallay).

Zorn, E. (2004), *Weaving a Future: Tourism, Cloth, and Culture on an Andean Island* (Iowa City: University of Iowa Press).

Notes on Contributors

Raul Acosta earned a doctoral degree in Social Anthropology from the Institute of Social and Cultural Anthropology, in the University of Oxford, in 2007. He is currently a post-doctoral research fellow at the Centre for Research on Applied Ethics, at the University of Deusto, in Bilbao, Spain. His research interests are activism, advocacy, political anthropology, transnational networks, environment, and urban issues. He has carried out research in Mexico, Brazil and Spain.

Sam Beck is the Director of the Urban Semester in New York City where he teaches ethnographic methods through an internship and community-service programme. He has carried out research in Yugoslavia, Iran, Romania and various parts of the United States. At present he is concerned with the intersection of ethnographic and experiential learning methods, university–community engagement and public scholarship, intergroup relations, and the political economy of North Brooklyn, New York City. He published *Ethnicity and Nationalism in Southeastern Europe* (co-edited with John W. Cole, Universiteit van Amsterdam, 1981) and *Manny Almeida's Ringside Lounge: The Cape Verdean Struggle for their Neighborhood* (Gávea-Brown Publications, 1992). He is currently working with a number of North Brooklyn community organizations in the capacity of a public anthropologist to create conditions of socio-cultural sustainability among Latinos who are being impacted by displacement, gentrification and the silencing of their history in this part of New York City. In collaboration with Los Sures United and Churches United he and his students helped establish El Museo de Los Sures people's museum.

Udi Mandel Butler is a research associate at the Institute of Social and Cultural Anthropology, University of Oxford, and a research fellow at the International Center for Research and Policy on Childhood (CIESPI) in Rio de Janeiro. Udi Butler's research has been mainly with children and young people living in a context of urban poverty in Rio de Janeiro, in particular those living on the street and in the *favelas*. A recent topic in this body of research looks at young people's perceptions of and engagement in public action in Brazil (NGOs, social movements, cultural groups, community organizations). On this theme, he has also conducted collaborative projects, through writing and photography, with young activists living in Rio's *favelas,* in association CIESPI. Udi is interested in different forms of collaborative research and in creative ways of communicating research. In line with this he has also worked with the Pitt Rivers Museum, University of Oxford, directing a number of ethnographic films which highlight the museum's collections and its relationships to source communities such as the Haida.

Thomas Hylland Eriksen is a professor of social anthropology at the University of Oslo. His research has mostly focused on the politics of identity and cultural aspects of globalization. Some of his books in English are *Ethnicity and Nationalism, Small Places, Large Issues* and *Globalization: The Key Concepts.* He has also written many books for a general readership, and argues for a public anthropology in *Toward Engaged Anthropology.*

Judith Goode is Professor of Anthropology and Urban Studies at Temple University. She is an urban anthropologist who uses ethnography to explore how the assumptions and techniques of post-Second World War policy in domains such as economic development, social provisioning, multiculturalism and immigration misrecognize the actual grounded knowledge and strategies of the people they are designed to help, thereby producing unintended contradictory results. She seeks to identify the specific contingent events, structures and cultural constructions at the local, national and global scale which produce these outcomes. Her ethnographic projects in Philadelphia since the 1970s are framed by the political economic trajectory of the city in the late twentieth century, especially in relation to the production of local space, and the shifting fault lines of the key axes of social difference and social movements. They seek to demonstrate how the national and global shift from the Keynesian welfare state to neoliberal privatization played out in this specific city and the consequences of this for governance, politics and political identities and action. She has co-authored or co-edited four books and many articles and has been an active leader in the formal institutionalization of urban anthropology, the anthropology of North America and the anthropology of policy.

BJ Isbell was initially trained in structuralism, symbolism and linguistics, and carried out research in Ayacucho, Peru, resulting in a classic ethnography, *To Defend Ourselves* (Waveland Press, 1985). She published a fictional account that dealt with the Shining Path web of violence she found there, *Finding Cholita* (University of Illinois Press, 2009). Her area of expertise is the Andean region of South America. Her current interests include: transgender is the U.S., ethnography and fiction, innovative technologies for teaching, and issues of global development and sustainability. She was the director of the Andean program for Cornell International Institute for Food, Agriculture and Development from 1990 until 2002. She also served as director of the Latin American Program at Cornell from 1987 to 1993 and again from 2001–2002.

Carl A. Maida is a professor in the Institute of the Environment and Sustainability at the University of California, Los Angeles. A medical anthropologist, he conducts ethnographic fieldwork on health and the environment in metropolitan Los Angeles. Previous publications include *Sustainability and Communities of Place* (Berghahn, 2011) *Pathways Through Crisis: Urban Risk and Public Culture* (Rowman and Littlefield, 2008), *Children and Disasters* (Routledge, 1999), and *The Crisis of Competence: Transitional Stress and the Displaced Worker* (Routledge, 1990). He is a fellow of the American Anthropological Association, the American Association for the Advancement of Science, and the Society for Applied Anthropology.

Brian McKenna, PhD, is a medical/environmental anthropologist and journalist with nearly two decades of experience as a public anthropologist. In the 1980s he worked in Philadelphia as a health policy analyst for a number of non-profits including Temple University's Institute for Public Policy Studies and the United Way's Community Services Planning Council. Later he had a stint as developmental specialist for NPR's Fresh Air. He worked for six years in medical education (1992–1998) as an evaluator for the Kellogg Foundation to create community-oriented primary-care practitioners, the topic of his dissertation. He has written for more than a dozen journalistic outlets including Lansing's *City Pulse*, where he wrote a weekly environmental health column. Other outlets include *Counterpunch, CommonDreams, The Free Press, The New York Guardian, Philadelphia City Paper* and Michigan's *Ecology Center*. McKenna coordinated a study on Lansing, Michigan's environmental health for the Ingham County Health Department between 1998 and 2001. In 2002 Brian received an environmental achievement award from the Ecology Center. He is currently writing a book entitled, *We all Live in Company Town USA*. Brian teaches at the University of Michigan-Dearborn.

Index

www.ingramcontent.com/pod-product-compliance
Lightning Source LLC
Chambersburg PA
CBHW060042030426
42334CB00019B/2442